Sea Lavender

Mike Herd

Sea Lavender

ISBN 978 1 7394728 1 8

First paperback edition 2023
Published by Scope Publishers.

Also by this author

Sea Lavender
Niobium
Justice for Lydia
No Tears for Destiny
The Medusa Shield
The Spirit of Askival

Sea Lavender

'The capacity of human memory is infinite.'

It was dark, hot and claustrophobic. Shapeless forms slowly emerged that were fuzzy and out of focus. The sounds were frightening. Rapid breathing, a heartbeat, regular, continuous, dependable but the clarity of the muscular movement and the whooshing of blood was astonishingly vivid. Other more muffled sounds were filtering through, predominately screeching and whooping. Pressure a strong muscular pressure, guiding, pushing and then there was light. A blinding searing white light and the whooping and screeching became unbearably loud. The shapeless became shapes. The first touch of mother and daughter as Giselle felt strong but gentle hands and arms holding her. Eyes adjusted and focussed on the large round face of a proud Bonobo mother nuzzling and kissing her. Giselle looked round to see another two in attendance acting as if they were midwives. They were in a nest of leaves high up in the crown of a tree. Giselle looked on as mother and midwives ate the placenta. A nearby colony of great egrets noisily chattered and a flock of African grey parrots flew over wings whirring.

Clouds formed from nowhere in the deep blue sky. White wispy cotton clouds growing bigger and joining with others, darkened the sky. Giselle felt the wind gather. A powerful dust filled wind that blew through the tree bending its branches one way and then the other. The wind slowly subsided as a distant rumble echoed through the forest. A flash of lightning preceded a loud crack of thunder. Giselle hung on in fear as the three Bonobos hugged each other protecting her as rain fell and in seconds it was torrential. A heavier than usual tropical rain storm cascaded down on the group. One of them picked up a large broad leaf and held it above them in vain. Giselle shivered with the sudden change in temperature. The downpour stopped as quickly as it had started and the sun broke through warming the chilled Bonobos. They shook to rid themselves of the water sending silver droplets into the air. Wisps of steam wafted gently upwards from them. Giselle's head was pushed towards her mother's warm wet breast and suckling noises could be heard. A warble fly buzzed around the group causing alarm and much swiping until it left.

Human voices penetrated the forest, shouting, aggressive voices that had no respect for its sanctity. The egrets went quiet. An eerie tense silence ended with a rifle shot. The whine of the bullet was clearly audible passing overhead, then another and another. The egrets flew off flapping their wings loudly. Giselle clung to her mother and looked sideways to see the other two Bonobos leading the way through the forest canopy at speed. More shots rang out from the forest below. Giselle was thrown from her mother onto a clump of moss and hung on watching as her mother fell hurtling downwards a hundred and thirty feet below into the darkness of the undergrowth.

Doctor Elizabeth Graham staggered back at the impact of what she was viewing, her hands shaking as she took off the Virtual Reality Headset. Pulling back the tight hood of her thermo-sensitive pressure suit, released her long red hair. She stopped the clock on the monitor and sat down transfixed with what she had just seen. She could not believe the images that were coming directly from Giselle's earliest memories. It had actually worked. Tears stung her freckled cheeks and the adrenaline coursing through her system made her feel sick. Elizabeth reached into her handbag taking out a mirror and a tissue. She dabbed her eyes put on her glasses and pushed aside her hair. Giselle the bonobo now nearly six years old was sedated, lying on a trolley wearing what looked like a shower cap with connected wires. She was found in a forest in the equatorial Democratic Republic of Congo by primatologists from the Harrison Dale Institute for Evolutionary Anthropology. Bonobos or pygmy chimps share 98.7% of the same DNA as humans, ideal for Elizabeth's research. She was shaking, not just because she had shared an intimate experience with Giselle, not just that she had witnessed appalling cruelty but also because the trials had succeeded beyond her wildest dreams. She decided not to press Giselle any further in case there were unforeseen side effects and put the system on standby.

Doctor Graham's seven years of hard work was going nowhere until she stumbled on a paper written by an Icelandic theoretical geneticist on DNA memory. Professor Christel Hilmarsson argued that the brain came pre-wired with skills and memories inherited from previous generations almost like a computer operating system. Savants are people who are prodigies having "natural" skills far beyond their teaching. The paper allowed Elizabeth to alter her conceptual computer model while maintaining its integrity. She took a deep breath and fought to keep her emotions in check, emotions that were uncommon for her, childish excitement, anxiety, apprehension and disbelief. She would have to do more tests before she could go public. Wearing a one piece pressure and temperature sensitive suit and hood she had felt every movement from Giselle's memory. She was Giselle. Elizabeth steadied herself and reached forward pressing her touch screen. A colleague in a white coat appeared.

"Frank, could you collect Giselle? I'm going to give her a little rest for now."

Elizabeth tapped the screen icon twice. The familiar face of Professor Daniel Stanford CBE and head of the Neurological Research Centre appeared. In his late thirties and only a few years older than Elizabeth, he was clearly pleased to see her. Clean shaven, relatively young for a professor and good looking, his shiny dark hair was combed back. He always wore a leather handmade waistcoat over a crisp white shirt and brown tie. A matching fedora hung on a hat stand behind him ready for when he left the office.

"Elizabeth good you're still here, I thought you might have gone."

Elizabeth had an elbow on the desk with her chin resting in the palm. She stared at the image on the screen.

"Are you Ok?" he asked

"Dan come up I must see you right away, it's very important."

"Ok, I've just had a strange call from the Security Intelligence Services," he said. "They're sending some people round to talk to us this evening. He wouldn't say why. Maybe it's got something to do with your work."

"What? No I don't think so. If it is there is something weird going on. Anyway how could they know about my work? I haven't published anything yet and you know I work alone but the timing is very strange." She ended the link just as the door opened and Frank came in.

"Hey Dr Graham, how did it go?" he said cheerfully looking at his watch. "Do you want Giselle tomorrow?"

"It went unbelievably well my head is buzzing right now. Sorry it's late I forgot what the time was."

Elizabeth took off the sensor lined cap from Giselle.

"I'm, going to let her chill out for a while bring her up about eleven tomorrow."

"Come on my girl," he said guiding the trolley through the open door.

Elizabeth's laptop was synced with the mainframe server recording everything. She was looking for her digital diary on one of the three touch screens on her desk. She never quite understood why admin insisted that she had the three, it complicated things and her life was complicated enough. Her office on the top floor of the Neurological Research Centre in the heart of London was spacious and untidy. A bench along one wall was covered with bits of electronics, old computers that she didn't want to throw out, fossils from a holiday on the Sutherland coast and a pair of spelter elephant mystery clocks in poor condition. One day she would get round to cannibalizing one to restore the other. Above the bench was a single length of a cork noticeboard covered in photographs. Some of the reminders still pinned on it she had long forgotten about and hadn't removed. Fixed to the cork was a curious carved mahogany wall bracket in the shape of winged Putto that she had found in a skip. It supported an old tennis trophy won in her teens. The screen icon was blinking on her monitor. She tapped it to reveal an image of a smartly dressed sixty something woman.

"Hi Mum." Elizabeth put her hand over her open mouth. "Sorry I was just about to call you, happy birthday."

"Of course you were its lovely to see you Elizabeth. How are you, you're looking a little tired, have you been crying, are you eating Ok. It must be late in London..."

As she spoke Elizabeth saw her reflection on the screen. The heady adrenaline was wearing off and she was tired. All these years stretching the boundaries of theoretical neuroscience, not knowing if it would work, and now it had. The Remembrance Project teased apart the relationship between brain function and memory recall. Where was Daniel, she was desperate to tell him.

"...I bumped into your friend Jody yesterday," said her mother. "She's looking tired too who wouldn't with twins. Did I tell you she had twins, I can't remember."

Elizabeth leaned closer to the screen. "Have you done something to your hair? It's a different colour and you're looking like you're dressed to go out somewhere."

"Well I kind of let myself go a little since your father died and I thought... maybe it was time to enjoy looking at myself in the mirror again and I have a lunch date."

"Wow, you're seeing someone?"

Elizabeth's mother smiled. "Not really, it's Jeremy Boulter. Remember Jeremy? He was your fathers' lawyer. There are still a few loose ends to tie up and he wanted to make it an informal working lunch. I think he also remembered it was my birthday. But he is single and good looking and I think he quite likes me and who knows. Are you and Daniel still good friends? You know he worships you."

"Mum."

"Well I'm not getting any older and neither are you. I would like to be a grandmother sometime soon and he's only a few years older than you and very good looking..."

"Mum," Elizabeth heard her mothers' doorbell chime.

"Hold on sweetie, I'll be back in a minute."

Elizabeth closed her eyes and sighed, if she didn't tell somebody soon she would go crazy. She heard the door creek and opened her eyes. Daniel was standing there leaning against it holding his fedora hat with a smile on his face. At five foot eight and slightly built he could never be mistaken as an athlete.

"I've got some amazing news," she said waving him in.

"Have you?" he asked sitting down. "When I saw you just now on the link it looked like you'd had a shock. I was hoping we could maybe try that new Turkish restaurant along the road you know meat on the flaming sword at the table, and then maybe we could walk round to my flat. It's not very far."

"Oh wait a sec," she said looking at the empty image of her mother's living room. "Mum...Mum!" Elizabeth's mother appeared.

"Sorry dear Jeremy's just arrived, I've got to go. Take a few days off Elizabeth, go visit your cousin in Inverness with Pepper, Marie would be delighted to see you. Speak to you tomorrow."

Elizabeth breathed a sigh of relief as she ended the call and looked at her watch. "I hope my neighbour has fed Pepper."

"Do you fancy that?" he asked hopefully.

"What?"

"Egemen's Turkish restaurant."

"Daniel. I've done it," she said quietly.

"Done what?"

"I ran a test on Giselle this evening and I'm still shaking. I've been dying to tell you."

"No way?"

"I could see, hear and feel Giselle's memory it was as if I was there. I'll show you."

Elizabeth took the project server off pause and ran the recording.

"This is Giselle in her mother's womb. Isn't that extraordinary, I really can't believe it," she said.

Tears started forming again at the corners of her eyes as they watched Giselle's first sight of her mother. Dan put his arm around her and stared in astonishment. They watched in silence until the recording finished.

"That's astounding," he said. "I can hardly believe it. I can say this now, I never thought for a minute you had any chance of succeeding. In fact I was asked by the principal to re-evaluate your work. That's dip-lo speak for close it down. I don't know what to say. Congratulations Elizabeth. All that hard work has paid off." He stood up and took her in his arms. "You could be listed for a Nobel, and many other prizes too no doubt. You know I tend to give you guys freedom to work, especially when it's highly experimental. So it's just fantastic to see it come through successfully."

He released her and they sat down again looking at the still frame of the undergrowth that swallowed up baby Giselle's mother.

"I had plenty of doubts too believe me," she said.

"I don't understand. There are lots of research groups that have fairly conclusive evidence that memory is dynamic and changes every time it's accessed by the Temporal Lobe. How on earth did you manage it?"

"Yes that's correct but I think that it's because emotion plays a big part in creating and reconstructing memories but if you bypass the emotive consciousness, it's all there. Using the crude computer analogy, I am the operating system the temporal lobe is ram and the hard drive is the brain. By directly accessing the temporal lobe I can bypass conscious anxiety factors that can cause distortion. The more we struggle to remember something the more the brain can become predictive. It can bridge gaps reaching conclusions that never happened or are not real as in hallucinations. However you know there are two separate fields concerning memory. With DNA, memory code is written sequentially with four chemical nucleotides not dissimilar to the zeros and ones of conventional hard drives. That means that DNA memory could theoretically be consciously accessed. There is evidence suggesting that holocaust survivor's children's children still suffer from its effects. Our ancestor's successes, fears and life-saving habits that have been passed down thousands of years could give us an incredible insight into past generations. Even now it's possible to store vast amounts of memory on very small amounts of DNA. This is a fascinating field that might be a future project but that's not what Remembrance is. My focus and all the theoretical and practical work I have done has been entirely on personal memory. As you saw on the recording, primates start encoding memory early, even in the womb. Experiences triggered by senses, initially fall into the short term memory. The brain prefers a sequential coding similar to automation, it doesn't particularly want you to be thinking all the time about everything you do. Once a pianist masters a piano he's not thinking about what his fingers are doing. If he tried to he wouldn't be able to play properly. It is encoded into long term memory. Somehow the brain sorts out what the important memories are and stores them in the implicit long term memory. But we do have a say over what we retain in the long term memory, by repetition for example. The brain also uses memory to make behavioural predictions. If you are in the wild and see a predator you will know what its intentions are or if you are in a city you have to make all kinds of predictions almost simultaneously. Imagination and memory use the 'default network' system. Based on ones experiences encoded in memory, one can imagine scenarios in the future where you will know precisely how you would react or even how someone else would behave. Emotive responses to memory are quite interesting too. Emotions like fear, sadness, embarrassment, pleasure, jealousy, love and hate encode indelibly and are just as easily retrieved. But I believe the brain sorts out long term memory as milestones in our past to keep us sane. You see the interesting thing is I don't believe it discards any memory at all, it's all still there."

Daniel ran his thumb along the leather band on his Fedora.

"Incredible. I did a course on hypnosis which was fascinating and I believe there was evidence of an increase in brain activity during the hypnotic state."

Elizabeth nodded. "Posthypnotic amnesia (PHA) used by hypnotists could be a temporary memory blocker and it's fascinating how auto-suggestions can alter ones perception of past reality but involuntary memory really puzzles me. Why would some obscure memory spring to mind unaided? What's going on there? I don't know." Elizabeth adjusted the glasses on her nose.

Daniel reached across and touched her arm. "There was a remarkable Harvard teacher in the nineteen seventies an artist who was also called Elizabeth, have you heard of her? Elizabeth was a pseudonym to hide her identity. This amazing woman could mentally project an exact image on to a canvass and paint it in the most exquisite detail, texture, shadow, colour, everything."

"That's right," said Elizabeth. "Charles Stromeyer III used a Julesz random-dot stereogram in a test. One eye was allowed to see a page of 10,000 dots for a length of time and then the other eye saw a different page with 10,000 dots. She was able to put the two pages together in her mind and drew the exact image from the composite of the two pages. It's quite astonishing. Sadly for science he married her and stopped researching her. I wonder if he ever did the test with her using both eyes. I would love to have met her. What she was able to do and my success with Giselle seems pretty conclusive that everything that you have ever done, seen, heard dreamed about is recorded somewhere in the brain. It explains how some people like Elizabeth have photographic memories. There are other different kinds of memory but essentially whether it's long or short term, memory it is recoverable. I started the project using a scaled down version of the functional magnetic resonance imaging (fMRI) equipment and Array Tomography which helped me to map in real time Synapses and connectomes. Have you ever flown over Buffalo City New York at night? It's just like that, a living illustration of the neural pathways. Then I focussed on activity to and from the Temporal Lobe. That acts like a gateway, an indexer and an accessor of memory again like the ram on a computer knows where data is stored and in what order. It can be accessed in an infinite multiplicity of different pathways."

Daniel walked slowly over and sat on the edge of her desk placing the Fedora on his knee. Elizabeth tapped his hat.

"There has been work done that suggests that early-response genes in the hippocampus have to be broken to allow learning and memory. These breaks are repaired quickly but the ability to repair them may deteriorate as we get older. And when we struggle to remember something it could also be because neurons in a well-used pathway have been lost and our struggle to remember is actually the Temporal Lobe trying to find another route. When it does find another route or more importantly if it does, we remember. It needs a lot more research but it may be possible that when new pathways are used it changes our perception of what actually happened in the past, creating new/old memories. There are a number of triggers that summon memory. A particular smell, a single word or phrase, a piece of music, a taste, even touch in fact all the senses that were used to create memories can be instrumental in retrieving them. Before GPS certain areas of the brains of London taxi drivers were unusually large. Can you imagine what it would be like remembering where every street in London is?" Elizabeth took Daniel's hand. "I have to repeat the clinical trials but the Remembrance Project works. It has the potential to find and I believe that with more testing, it can delete memory. Just think what you could do with that? My degree on Neuroscience included Psychology at Aberdeen and that was invaluable. The possibilities are endless. A traumatic event stays with you for the rest of your life but now it's treatable. This will cure it. Soldiers returning from war zones who have witnessed the most horrible events imaginable take with them post-traumatic stress disorder, nightmares, flashbacks, depression, suicide; they can be free of all these memories. Any trauma victims damaged by near death experiences can recover completely. By selectively deleting traumatic memories it is entirely possible to restore innocence to abused children for example. They could start their lives anew getting back their childhood."

Elizabeth took a small bottle of water out of her bag and drank from it.

"It will help many, many patients with brain damage affecting memory including Alzheimer sufferers, by finding new pathways and stimulation."

Daniel's eyebrows went up. "Do you really think so?" he asked.

"Yes, I do." Elizabeth smiled. "How is your father?"

"Getting worse, that was one of the reasons that I first became interested in neurology."

"I know I'm sorry Dan," Elizabeth sighed. "But that's not all it can do it has the potential to allow police access to memory crime scenes. They would be able to have accurate witness memory videos to check evidence and find criminals. There would be no need for trials because it would effectively be an admission of guilt if it was encoded in the criminals' memory. In fact crime would drop because those wishing to break the law would realize that they couldn't hide the past. Then there are addictions whether its drugs or alcohol. They are on two levels physical and mental. Mental addiction is far more serious and can take forever to overcome. Smokers for example can still dream about starting to smoke again many years after the body has rid itself of nicotine."

Elizabeth took another drink of water. "But... there are deep moral, ethical and potentially dangerous issues at stake here and I'm not sure if I'm qualified to make a judgement on it. There is another use that can't be ignored. It would be possible to militarise and weaponize Remembrance. Captured soldiers could potentially have their memories completely deleted leaving only procedural memory, how you walk and talk and breath and eat and so on. Theoretically they could 're-educate' them by pasting manufactured memories or even someone else's memories. They could integrate them into armies. Political dissidents could be treated similarly. It could be the catalyst for triggering global authoritarianism way beyond George Orwell's wildest nightmares. I am very worried. It could be used for evil as well as good. What do I do now?"

"How secure is your data and programming?" asked Daniel.

"Well..." Elizabeth stopped when there was a knock on the door. It opened and a woman with a reddish face wearing a cream coat and matching handbag peaked round the door.

"Sorry to interrupt professor but there are some people asking to see you, they said they were expected."

"Show them to the conference room Jill and could you bring some tea and biscuits please. I'm sure I could do with a cup." Jill gave Elizabeth a look and left.

"I could do with something stronger but that's going to have to wait," he said. "In my experience Elizabeth I think you are at a stage where you need a great deal of support from the government and very soon. You need assistance in insuring security and built in safe guards. Is it possible for example to hard-wire a specific use for Remembrance?"

"It may be possible using quantum mechanics to make replication impossible at an atomic level but I doubt it. If I couldn't, I don't know how Remembrance could be made available for even specialized use without it falling into the wrong hands. I have to take off this pressure-sensitized jump suit. Off you pop and see your spooks I'll be along in a minute."

"I don't mind waiting."

"You should be so lucky you know I don't wear anything under this."

Mrs Annette Davidson put on a red cardigan, her favourite and rummaged around in a drawer until she found the Yale key. She took off her sheepskin lined slippers and put on her "sensible" shoes her son had bought after her last fall just before her eightieth birthday. The door closed and locked with a click on her modest terraced house in Batter-sea. It was getting dark but the street lights hadn't come on yet. Three women skimpily dressed for clubbing were passing.

"Hello Netta, we're off to the SinBin are you coming?"

"I can't dear, I have to feed my neighbours' cat. Are you not frightened you'll catch your death of cold?"

They laughed and kept on walking. The key turned easily in the lock of the blue door and swung open. Netta sniffed the air subconsciously and closed the door. She could hear Pepper growling in the kitchen.

"I'm coming Pepper," she said. "You naughty puss."

Pepper was in a green cat carrier on the work top next to a tall well-dressed man in a suit holding a mobile phone. Netta picked up a frying pan by the handle with both hands swinging it over her left shoulder and advanced towards him.

"Who are you and what are you doing with Pepper?" she asked.

"And you would be?"

"I would be Mrs Davidson to you."

"Well put the frying pan down Mrs Davidson. I wouldn't want you to be arrested for assaulting a police officer."

2

'As distasteful as it is, I think we
are only faced with one answer.'

It started to rain. The wiper blades on the yellow cab made an annoying sound as they moved across the wind shield. The radio hissed and crackled while orders were given out from HQ and the heating was a little too high. The cab sped along the US 40 in Baltimore heading for Focacceria Alberto on Eastern Avenue. The Sikh driver, wearing a light blue Dastar covering his head, had been born and raised in Baltimore. He glanced in the mirror at Ruby and Jeremy.

"This used to be known as the highway to nowhere," he said shaking his head. "I've been to Alberto's. You'll enjoy it, we did. They have great pizzas. I took my wife on our anniversary. What time do you want to be picked up? Don't matter; call me 15 minutes before you want to leave."

The traffic was busier than usual at this time of day making it easier for the large nondescript black saloon to follow them.

"The lasagne is good as well, that's what my wife had but whoosh its jolly expensive. This must be a special occasion, yes."

The cab driver was used to having rhetorical conversations with passengers. Sometimes he talked like that to his wife at home until she gave him a look. The cab pulled up outside the restaurant and the following car parked behind. Jeremy paid the driver giving him a generous tip and the rain eased a little as they got out. Waiting on the side-walk were two men in suits wearing earpieces with tell-tale cords.

"Mrs Ruby Graham, I'm agent Ross and this is agent Stenner," he said showing his ID. "Can we talk to you in private?"

"Excuse me gentlemen I'm Jeremy ..."

"...Boulter," agent Ross interrupted, "Attorney at law. Believe me sir it is extremely important that we talk with Mrs Graham in private."

He led Ruby away by the arm while agent Stenner waited for a moment and then followed. Ruby and Ross got into the back of the car while Stenner sat behind the wheel.

"What's this all about?" asked Ruby.

"All I can tell you for now is that we have good reason to believe that your life is in danger."

The engine fired up and they took off leaving Jeremy standing outside Alberto's as they headed back to the road to nowhere.

Lit by a series of filtered strip lights it was small by normal boardroom standards but more comfortable and it had the smell of a new carpet. Three men and a woman stood up when Professor Stanford followed by Doctor Graham entered. As they reached out to shake hands the thin one in a grey suit spoke.

"I am Maurice Wells and this is my colleague Andrew Speight from the Secret Intelligence Service (SIS), Caroline Trent and Chase Wilson are from the CIA."

Jill still wearing her coat knocked at the door and came in with a tray and put it on the table. "I'll see you tomorrow professor," she said.

"Thanks Jill."

The agents sat down and waited until she left, closing the door. "Doctor Graham..."

"...Tea anyone?"

Daniel interrupted pouring out a cup. There was a chorus of no thank you.

"Professor, are you fully familiar with Dr Graham's research?" asked Maurice Wells.

Daniel helped himself to a mug of tea.

"Well the purpose and benefits of research has to be clear if we are to get funding of course and so I do know about Elizabeth's work but only on the periphery and only on the objectives, not on the procedure. We normally have a monthly catch-up. Elizabeth and I have an understanding. I'm always available if she needs any advice or help and I give her space to do her job."

Maurice Wells scratched his head and looked at Daniel. "In that case in the interests of your security our conversation with Doctor Graham must be in private. It would be best to keep you in the dark sir. In fact I think you should leave if you don't mind."

Daniel looked at Elizabeth. "It's Ok," she said

"What about eating?"

"I'm not really hungry Dan, might just grab something later."

"Are you sure?" he replied.

Elizabeth nodded and gave him a smile. He turned pushed his chair under the table picked up the mug of tea and a biscuit said goodbye and left. Caroline Trent was dressed in a blue suit with a grey cravat pinned with a platinum and diamond brooch in the shape of a butterfly. She put a notepad on the table and opened it.

"It's been confirmed that CIA servers in Langley Virginia were hacked and a great many gigabytes of files stolen. We haven't even got the slightest clue who or how. It could be the Russians, Chinese, North Koreans or even an unholy alliance of all three. These files put at risk agents, contacts and..." she hesitated. "...on-going sensitive projects."

"What does that have to do with me? Wait a minute, you mean on-going projects like mine?" asked Elizabeth."

"Yes we have files on your project."

There was a silence broken by Elizabeth tapping the table.

"How could you have my files? I don't understand. There are not many people who know what I am working on." Elizabeth was beginning to get a little angry. "What am I supposed to say? You come here to tell me that you illegally possess files from my computer having hacked into it."

Agent Trent shifted in her seat. "Ma'am the CIA has not hacked into your computer."

Wells studied the palms of his hand.

"How did you get them?" asked Elizabeth.

"I'm sorry Doctor Graham I'm not in a position to give you that information."

Elizabeth pursed her lips "Well in any case they're all encrypted and even if they were decrypted I'm the only one that could make sense of the construction order of the computer model."

"Well that makes you uniquely valuable and at the same time extremely vulnerable."

"Let me just get this straight you're here to tell me that somebody has an illegal copy of an illegal copy of Remembrance and you think I could be a target."

"Yes."

"The only way you could have had the faintest idea about my project is if it was decrypted. Look if you want my cooperation I need some answers."

"I believe the opening preface was decrypted." Maurice Wells cleared his throat. "Everybody is hacking everybody. America is hacking China, China is hacking Russia and America and goodness knows who else, everybody it seems. It's going on all the time. Even companies that sell hacking software to governments are getting hacked."

His mobile buzzed. He took it out and put it on the table. "Dr Graham as an American citizen we have a duty to ensure your safety and that of your immediate family, you're lives are all at serious risk. Agent Trent has already taken steps to ensure the safety of Mrs Graham. If you and the project you are working on falls into the wrong hands and that would be virtually any nation on this planet that is not democratically governed, it could change the course of humanity as we know it."

Caroline Trent put her hand flat on the table. "Whoever hacked into our servers will already know about your project and its potential. The encryption on the preface in particular was out of date. Arrangements have been made to take you and your equipment to a secure location where you can work safely and unhindered." Agent Trent's phone received a text.

"No." Elizabeth dug her heels in. "I'm not at all comfortable with just disappearing if you don't mind I'll take my chances. I have too many commitments."

Andrew Speight's phone rang. He listened looking directly at Elizabeth and ended the call. "There's a rapid response team with a police motorcycle escort waiting outside, believe me Dr Graham we wouldn't be going to these lengths for fun," he said.

"Wait this is all happening too fast I can't just disappear and then there's my cat."

Wells shrugged. "It's all being taken care of. It's best you don't go home."

"What about my mother?"

"I've just had a text confirming that Mrs Graham is heading for a safe house with round the clock protection," said Trent.

"Safe? But I was only talking to her a few minutes ago."

"I know," she said.

"I'd better get my things together," said Elizabeth.

They all stood up. "No need Dr Graham it's all in hand. May I have your mobile," asked Wells.

"I don't have any choice, do I?" Elizabeth's question hung in the air.

The silence was replaced by a humming, whirring sound. A black almost invisible reconnaissance class optic-drone hovered outside the window. On board a real time satellite linked 4k digital camera using face recognition accurately identified everyone in the room within three seconds before it disappeared.

Trent turned to Wells. "Was that one of yours?"

"No," he replied putting his hand to a lapel. "This is Wells, there's a spy drone in the area, shoot it on sight. Come on we must go now."

A loud explosion on the floor above shook the building and cascaded ceiling tiles and plaster onto them. "My lab," shouted Elizabeth.

"Let's get out of here," said Wells.

Waiting outside was a black limousine and two backup vehicles surrounded by a highly trained heavily armed emergency response team. Four police motorcycle outriders with blue flashing lights nervously revved their engines. Caroline Trent bundled Elizabeth into the back seat while Speight and Wells went into the front seats. Chase Wilson took the wheel of one of the backups. Above, on an adjacent flat topped roof twenty semi-autonomous military grade swarm-drones mounted with recoilless and silenced laser guided weapons took off. Covered with a special black paint that absorbs 99% of light leaving them invisible with only what appeared to be, black holes in the sky. They swooped down buzzing like angry bees, laser lights strafing and firing on their surprised targets. A one sided fire fight ensued with the loss of all the rapid response team and the police motorcyclist in a terrifyingly short time. It was like a war zone with bodies everywhere.

A mini RPG loaded drone targeted the backup car and let loose a rocket that blew Chase Wilson's car ten feet up in the air covered in flames. Two swarm-drones hovered one on either side of Maurice Wells and Andrew Speight. Before they could get their guns out, synchronized shots were fired from each drone through the window killing them instantly. A tall black helmeted motorcyclist pulled up and put a fist through the window shattering it. Caroline Trent covered in tiny fragments of glass was ready to respond and fired a shot at the chest. The bullet bounced off and before she could react the motorcyclist opened the door from the inside, pulled her out of the car and threw her fifteen yards, landing on the chassis of the upturned back-up car. The bike rider lifted the visor to reveal a young attractive black woman's face. She pulled Elizabeth who was screaming and struggling effortlessly out of the car as a driverless gyro stabilized two wheeled pod stopped next to them. She slid open the door and pushed Elizabeth in, closing it swiftly with a clunk. It moved off turning into a busy main street negotiating the traffic.

The killer swarm-drones had gone leaving the optic-drone tracking high up observing all below. Elizabeth tried the door but it was locked. She kicked it as hard as she could to no avail. The shooting and bombing seemed to have gone on forever to Elizabeth but in fact it was all over in a matter of minutes. Hearing sirens she looked back and saw several police cars with blue lights flashing in full chase. The optic-drone still tracking above began to emit bursts of digital audio on a DAB frequency. The DAB carried hacking computer code gaining access through the pursuing cars infotainment and took control of the steering, brakes and accelerator. The patrol cars were gaining on Elizabeth when one turned left straight into a shop front. Two more simply slammed on the breaks and as Elizabeth's driverless pod turned right, the following pack just kept going straight on. Elizabeth thought the world was going mad then she heard an odd hissing sound accompanied by a slightly familiar odour and began to feel very sleepy.

Daniel climbed up the stairs of the tube station carrying a bag containing a take away from an Indian restaurant and walked the hundred or so yards to his apartment. He was haunted by those images from Giselle and how, what had happened to her in the Congo explained her odd behaviour when she first came to the NRC. Any loud bangs and she would hide inside Frank's white coat shivering. It took a great deal of patience and trust. But part of him still couldn't quite believe the enormity of Elizabeth's research. The intervention by the security services was probably the best thing for her. She would be safe with government protection. He punched in the entry code and climbed the stairs avoiding the small lift that was a little claustrophobic. The flat was depressingly quiet. It was neat and tidy and orderly and empty. His cleaning lady was a great find but in truth she didn't have much to do, he hardly spent much time here since Rhona left him. He switched on the TV and chose a news channel more for company than the news. It was usually doom and gloom anyway. He sat on the sofa and opened the container lid. The aroma of the very hot Laal Maas take away was wonderful. He first tasted this spiciest of dishes in Rajasthan while touring India with Rhona just after they were married and every time he ate the dish memories of happier times briefly returned. He always wondered how people living in one of the hottest places on the planet came to concoct such a fiery dish. The TV sound was quite low and Daniel, wholly absorbed in his lamb curry, failed to see the images of the emergency vehicles, flashing blue lights and rushing ambulances on the screen. He went to the fridge and took out a cold beer returning to the sofa.

Glancing at the screen a caption read '*live at the scene.*' and at the bottom of the picture it had a strap line saying, '*A number of security personnel gunned down in Breckinridge Avenue London.*' There was a reporter giving a live piece to camera near the location. Daniel grabbed the TV remote and turned up the sound.

"...Police have said that at least nine people have been found dead so far but it's likely that the death toll will rise even further. The bodies of eight men and a woman have been recovered and their identities will be withheld until relatives have been notified." Daniel stood up his mouth open staring at the screen. "Metropolitan Commissioner Sir Robert Mayhew said that this is a rapidly changing on-going incident and it is still too early to determine whether it is a terrorist attack. He added that as yet no terrorist groups have claimed responsibility. This is without doubt one of the bloodiest gun battles ever to occur in London."

Daniel's face was ashen white. He picked up his mobile and clicked on Elizabeth's number. It kept ringing and just when he was about to give up Daniel was shocked to hear a male voice answer.

"Hello."

"Who's that? Where's Elizabeth?"

"Who is this?"

"Professor Daniel Stanford, why have you got Elizabeth's phone?"

The line went dead. The buzzer from the outdoor entry system sounded. Daniel walked over to the security pad and pressed a button. He could see two men.

"Yes?"

"Professor Stanford it's important you come with us. It's very urgent," said one holding an identity card to the camera.

A big convention was taking place at the CIA's Scattergood–Thorne Centre in Langley. The large old two and a half story white painted wooden mansion had a fleet of identical black chauffeur driven cars dropping their passengers off at the front door. The house on the campus was mostly used for conferences. On the third floor a small group of men sat round an angled touch screen in silence. They were watching CCTV images courtesy of GCHQ of the swarm-drone battle in London. It was hardly a battle more of a calculated bloodbath as the drones chose their targets carefully and quickly dispatching each one. Lee Booker, the Director of the Central Intelligence Agency tapped the screen and the picture froze.

"What's that?" he said. It was the motorcyclist pulling up next to Elizabeth's car. He ran it forward in slomo. The door of the car opened. There was a flash from a gun inside the car. Booker stopped the image.

"How did Caroline miss at point blank range?"

The image began running again showing a large explosion as the RPG hit the car behind, landing on its roof. Caroline Trent was being pulled out of the car and thrown, landing on the upturned car behind.

"Wow, that's impossible, what are we dealing with here?" he said angrily. "The quality of this CCTV is shocking. Wait." He stopped the motion again.

The women had slid up the visor on her helmet. "Damn, there's hardly any detail. That's odd I don't see a face." They saw Elizabeth pulled into the pod and disappear. Lee looked round the table. "Any ideas guys, we could do with some right now."

Roy Pearson, Directorate of Analysis spoke first. "Two drones were shot down. We've received a report from Porton Down on one of them. It's not commercially available and it's highly sophisticated. They're called swarm-drones because the way they are programmed is based on the swarm principle where the drones are aware of each other in some kind of co-ordination, very impressive. That means it's likely to be a government that has a great deal of knowledge and resources and it's very unlikely to be a criminal gang."

"So who are we looking at, Russia, China?" asked Booker.

"Who knows maybe North Korea," said Pearson.

"Are the Trent and Wilson families being looked after?" asked Booker.

"They will be sir," said Aldo Johansen Directorate of Support.

"Good, Good," he said.

"So what do we know about this Doctor Graham?"

Roy tapped his tablet. "Elizabeth Heather Graham, thirty two years old born in Aberdeen Scotland. The only child of Ruby, a US national and George Alexander Graham Scottish, she has dual nationality. They left Scotland when Elizabeth was five for Seattle where she was educated to High School level. She travelled back to Scotland and received a BSc (Hon) in Neuroscience with Psychology at the University of Aberdeen. She then received her Doctorate in the field of Neuropharmacology & Cellular Neuroscience and presently works at the Neurological Research Centre in London. Her father died of a heart attack just over a year ago. We have a copy of her files from GCHQ and we've only managed to decipher a preface to her work. According to that Dr Graham was working on..."

"...What!"

"Um well she was working on some highly improbable project..."

"...Go on."

"Eh, a project called Remembrance which is designed to access human memory."

There was silence.

"You're kidding."

Roy shook his head. "Incidentally these files were copied and taken along with other files when our servers were hacked into."

"That's interesting do you think there could be a connection?"

"Could be Lee but that trail has gone cold."

"Ok so what have we got? A Doctor working on an as yet theoretical experiment is kidnapped by someone who has advanced drone capability, who badly wants her and it's possibly the same people who hacked into the CIA. There can't be too many options here guys."

The whirring sounds of a helicopter hovered noisily outside.

"This is a serious failure of the intelligence community. I'm going to have the President breathing down my neck for answers." Lee went to the window as it landed. He looked at his watch. "What are the chances that she pulled it off?"

"Sub-zero." A ripple of laughter went round the table.

"Mm, someone's gone to an awful lot of trouble for nothing if she hasn't. Is Hollinger available? We need some up to date information."

"He's at a COBRA meeting."

COBRA, the Cabinet Office Briefing Room A at 70 Whitehall, was lit with a central panel of strip lights. Closed, heavy bomb proof curtains covered rippled glass windows to counter laser microphone eavesdropping. Twenty dark leather chairs surrounded a long light coloured wooden table and at the far end of the room, eight video panels filled the wall space. On the table was the second drone shot down. Prime Minister Simon Phillips and his deputy were already there sitting at the head of the table. He was looking through some hastily scribbled briefing notes that they had received earlier as heads of the security services anti-terrorist experts and armed forces trooped in taking their seats. "This is a shambles, an absolute shambles." The Prime Minister face was red and angry. "Sir Anthony this is a very serious security failing, I'm already ordering an inquiry into why the security services had no knowledge of this impending attack. Do you have an update?"

Sir Anthony Hollinger the Director General of SIS the Secret Intelligence Service avoided looking at the PM and studied his notes. "Yes Prime Minister, ten members of the armed response team, four police officers, two SIS servicemen and two CIA agents, eighteen people dead and we are completely in the dark. These agents didn't have a chance. Whoever did this has knowledge of advanced robotics, electronics and very clever hacking tools. Of the two drones that were shot done one has been sent to Porton Down. It appears that these are semi-autonomous drones that communicate with each other and act rather like a large swarm of bees. They were in encrypted communication with a geostationary satellite and we don't yet know which one, that was relayed to a control server we don't know where. The electronics of the pursuit cars were hacked into by an optic-drone causing the drivers to lose control. There are two men from one patrol car in intensive care. It appears that all of these people died so that Dr Elizabeth Graham could be kidnapped."

The prime minister pointed to his public relations manager Gordon Coutts. "Gordon I think it would be best if we don't release anything about Doctor Graham's kidnapping for now. Why would anyone want to kidnap a Doctor working on experimental neurological research? It seems that I don't have all the facts yet, Anthony. I think we need to find her and fast. Find her and we've found the perpetrators." The PM pressed a button on an intercom on his desk. "Has Professor Stanford arrived yet, yes? Show him in please." Daniel looking bewildered walked in and was beckoned to an empty chair. The PM took off his glasses and looked at him. "Professor what I'm going to tell you must be kept in the strictest confidence, Doctor Graham is missing. She's been kidnapped. We need to find her quickly and we're hoping you can help. There may be something that she might have said or you may have some idea where she might be, possibly a country that has experimental neuroscientific researchers."

Daniel was stunned. He looked round the room at a sea of anonymous faces and his gaze settled on the drone. "I, I can't believe it. I called her mobile about twenty minutes ago and a man answered."

"That was one of our agents." said Hollinger. "We found Elizabeth's phone on Maurice Wells' body. Are there any countries that would specifically target Doctor Graham to advance their research?"

"There are Neuroscience and Experimental Psychology Institutes in most countries and I dare say that work is being done in the field of experimental neuroscience by the military as well, like the Defence Advanced Research Projects Agency in America. In fact DARPA wanted Elizabeth to join their team researching Transcranial Magnetic Stimulation of the temporal lobe with an electromagnetic field and Transcranial pulsed ultrasound. The former radically alters perception, making people believe things that they wouldn't normally and the latter was to be fitted into the latest development in mood bending sound waves inside troop combat helmets. They obviously didn't know Elizabeth, she turned them down flat. Neuroscience is a burgeoning field with a lot of interest. For example the University of Regensburg's Experimental and Clinical Neurosciences course enrol 50% of their students from all over the world."

"American R&D budget is $63.3 billion dollars and our R&D budget is 5.3 billion," said Defence Minister Murray Greig shifting in his seat.

The Prime Minister glared at him turning to Daniel. "Professor, any thoughts at all about Doctor Graham's whereabouts."

Daniel touched a rotor on the drone. "I have absolutely no idea where she might be. I suppose there are always possibilities that could be examined. She may well have been in communication with other scientists in the same field but, I think that's extremely unlikely because she always worked alone, preferred it that way."

"What about colleagues or acquaintances?"

Daniel leaned forward and looked at the tip of the small rotor blade. "Well she was working on something quite unique. How anyone could have known about it beats me because she hasn't published anything yet. I knew very little myself until today."

"Anthony I'm still not clear in my mind exactly what this is all about," said the PM.

"GCHQ has partially decrypted files suggesting that in the course of her work, Dr Elizabeth Graham was working towards a remarkable and some might say dangerous discovery. She may have developed a method of reading memories." There was a stunned silence. "Not just read them but see and hear everything. We don't know if It has been proved in clinical trials yet. Imagine being able to access someone's complete memory, every second of every minute of every hour, day, month, year...someone's whole life. Not just the bits that you and I can remember but every single second of one's life recorded and waiting to be played back like catch-up television. We retrieved the laptop from her lab. The hard drive was removed to bypass the login but we haven't been able to decrypt it. It seems that at some point she changed her encryption."

Daniel was aghast. "How on earth can you have a copy of Elizabeth's files and what right do you have taking NRC property?"

There was a silence in the room. "We are where we are professor," said Hollinger.

"The laptop belongs to my department and I would like it back immediately."

Hollinger sent an email on his tablet and got a reply almost immediately. "The laptop will be delivered to the NRC within the hour."

"Thank you," said Daniel looking closer at the drone. He saw etched into the rotor blade the image of an eagle. A shiver of anticipation raised the hairs on the back of his neck. "There were several people she knew some time ago who were kind of working on similar well not similar but parallel projects and one of them..."

Daniel stopped and withdrew his hand in horror. "What the hell..." The drone was melting into pools of liquid. Everyone stood up and moved back and someone opened a window. The drone had disappeared in front of their eyes and even the pools of liquid left were drying up. It was all over in a few seconds.

"Is everybody Ok?" asked the Prime Minister. They all nodded. "Murray exactly what just happened?"

The Defence Minister sat down and an aide whispered in his ear. "I believe DARPA has a project called ICARUS that could have a bearing but they're keeping us in the dark as they do about much of their research. There are over 5,000 patents kept secret in the patents office because publication might endanger national security."

The Chief of SIS interrupted. "Hopefully we still have the drone at Porton Down. Prime Minister there is a major issue here we have to consider, even without the laptop she may be able to re-create her work in another laboratory and that would be extremely dangerous and unacceptable. I cannot emphasize enough how catastrophic that would be."

Daniel leant back in his chair. He was shaken by what he had just seen and heard and instinctively knew that Elizabeth could have more than one enemy.

"Professor Stanford any ideas?" asked the PM.

"Um, I, I'm still in shock. She's not just a colleague she's a very close friend. When it came to her work there was never any need to confide in me. She was, is very independent." He stood up. "I'm sorry I can't help any further. Goodbye gentlemen, Prime Minister."

The door clicked shut. "That was a swift departure," said Hollinger. "Prime Minister, this is potentially disastrous for Western democratic countries. As distasteful as it is, I think we are only faced with one answer. We must destroy the project and the research and... while Doctor Graham is alive I'm afraid we are all at risk." A murmur went round the room.

The Chief of the Russian Foreign Intelligence Service (SVR) General Vladislav Golovanov was puzzled. He had seen television reports coming out of London and it made him think. The media were speculating that it was a terrorist attack but terrorists don't crack hard nuts they prefer soft easy targets. A coach, a train, a plane anywhere with concentrations of people, this was not a terrorist attack and there had been no electronic chatter, normally a precursor to an attack. Should Russia be concerned about this? He wasn't sure but the sophistication of the drones worried him. There was someone, some organization out there that had superior drone development and he had no idea who that could be. Russia's friends knew nothing therefore it was unlikely to be a government. So if you remove governments and terrorist groups, who could it possibly be and for what purpose?

3

"Have you ever been in a hot air balloon?"

"No."

Would you like to?"

"No."

"Why not? it's fun."

There was a loud humming sound adding to a dull headache behind her eyes. Elizabeth tried putting her hand up to her brow and couldn't. She opened her eyes and tried to move. Everything was blurred. She was strapped into a white leather passenger seat in a private jet. Completely disorientated, she was desperately trying to work out what happened to her when a door opened at the far end of the cabin and a shadowy figure walked towards her carrying a tray. As it got closer Elizabeth's vision improved recognizing the woman on the motorbike. She put the tray on the table in front of Elizabeth and sat opposite her. Her dark face and blond shoulder length hair curling at the end was quite striking.

"You killed all these people." said Elizabeth.

She lifted a cloth from the tray revealing a hypodermic syringe, a small phial and an antibacterial swab.

"What are you doing?" Elizabeth was getting scared.

The woman picked up the swab and rubbed Elizabeth's arm.

"Who are you?" she said straining at the straps.

The woman put it back on tray and picked up the hypodermic sticking it into the phial.

"Stop, I'm warning you." There was a sharp prick as the needle entered a vein. "Ow you'll pay for this." Elizabeth's head was beginning to spin. "Where are you taking me? Who are you working for? Why have you kidnapped me?"

The woman carefully put the syringe on the tray and covered it. She looked at her watch closed her eyes and leaned back in the chair.

"What time is it? Where's my wa..."

Daniel returned home. He turned on the television and went into his bedroom. Opening a cupboard he took out a new rucksack ripping off the plastic wrapping. It had been a present from his uncle in Devon in a baleful attempt to get him some real fresh air and exercise anywhere out of London. He unzipped a pouch at the bottom of the bag and put on an immaculate pair of walking boots, another present from his uncle, into the pouch and zipped it closed. He started packing clothes in a seemingly random way from a drawer. He was never very good at packing. Then the phone rang. “Professor it’s Jill are you Ok? I can’t believe what’s happening here. It wasn’t until I was on the tube that I discovered I’d left my door keys. The whole area’s been cordoned off. There’s ambulances and blood everywhere. I managed to get in through the green door and there’s been an explosion in Dr Graham’s lab. Computers and servers are all gone. What’s been happening?”

“Jill, I can’t explain right now but the news is speculating that it was a terrorist attack. I don’t mind admitting I am very shaken by what’s happened. I think I might take a few days leave, go to Scotland maybe do some fishing. This has been very difficult for me. What about Elizabeth’s laptop?”

“I saw it on your office desk.”

“Could you bring it round? By the way I would like to take the monopoly game with me. You know the one in the right hand bottom drawer of my desk? Do you remember the last time we played? I only beat you by £1000 if only it was real.” There was a short pause.

“I’m on my way,” she said.

“You’re a gem. When I get back remind me to speak to the Principle about giving you a pay rise. Bye Jill.”

In a darkened communications room at the Government Communication Headquarters, (GCHQ) two intelligence officers are studying the image of Professor Stanford putting the phone down. “What do you make of that?” asked the man.

“So he likes fishing and playing monopoly and he’s going off on a break because he’s upset.” His colleague shrugged her shoulders.

"Monopoly. His building has been attacked, staff kidnapped and he's wanting to play Monopoly, do me a favour you don't buy that do you? I don't. It sounded more like he was trying to tell her something knowing he could be bugged. He worked for us once remember."

"That's why you and I always end up working together. You're the paranoid conspiracy theorist and I'm the sensible one."

Her colleague snorted. "Oh really, well who do you think single-handedly foiled that plot to blow up the underground at rush hour Mm? I get paid for being paranoid it's what I'm good at. Suspect everyone; question everything never take anything at face value."

The flickering image of Daniel packing his rucksack, held their attention when the doorbell went. He left the room and returned with Jill who was carrying a small leather bag and the laptop. "That was quick. Thanks Jill would you like a cup of tea," he said packing the laptop into has rucksack.

"No thanks professor it's getting late and I have to get home."

Daniel kissed her on the cheek and she left. He put the curry into the microwave and switched it on and took a fresh beer out of the fridge.

Elizabeth opened her eyes. It was completely dark and silent. She wondered for a moment if she was in some kind of coma. She raised herself on her elbows triggering a motion sensor. Light appeared on the ceiling reflected from a giant aquarium with many species of tropical fish embedded into a wall. The room was windowless, clean and furnished. The bed was contained within a random geometrical matrix of chrome rods and had a black duvet facing a curved far wall. There was a white bedside shelf with her glasses, a small white table with no legs jutting out from the wall and two seats either side also fixed to the wall. Set into the wall above the table was a flush door with a touch panel. Her watch and clothes had gone and she was wearing a one piece cotton jumpsuit. She swung her legs over and touched the floor with her feet. An attempt to stand made her feel dizzy and she momentarily held on to a crossbar and sat down again. She waited a moment before trying it again. There were two doors on opposite walls without handles. She stood up and walked to the aquarium holding out her hand to touch it. It was warm. She closed her eyes.

"Elizabeth?" At the open door was the woman with blond hair.

Elizabeth jumped. "Where am I?" She asked leaning against the aquarium.

"My name is Jani. You are perfectly safe no harm will come to you." Her voice was rich and mellow and her perfect English had a slight east African accent.

"Why have I been taken here, am I a prisoner?"

"You are a guest, your life was in danger but now you are safe, you will not be harmed here." The woman touched a button on her Holovue wrist band and hidden lights faded up. "You must be hungry, what would you like? You can have anything you wish."

"What time is it?"

Jani looked at her watch. "5.16pm."

Elizabeth sat down next to the table shook her head and gestured. "Oh I don't know how about a steak? "she said sarcastically.

The woman walked over to the table, swiped at the touch pad and considered the images and options. She pressed the screen a few times and sat down opposite Elizabeth. It began to make a whirring, humming sound. Elizabeth studied her properly for the first time. She was quite tall and under the lustre black one piece jump suit, was an outline that was unmistakably of someone in perfect shape. She remembered the way the woman had effortlessly removed and thrown the CIA agent and the firm grip she had on her as she was propelled into the pod. But there was something odd about her that Elizabeth couldn't quite put her finger on. There was a ping and the door opened to reveal a perfect 3d printed and cooked steak with fries on a paper plate. The woman took them out and put them on the table. Elizabeth was surprised how good it was. Jani tapped the wall opening a panel to reveal a mini-bar. She walked over to the far door and a sensor opened it immediately revealing a completely white bathroom and shower.

"There is everything you might need here including clothes."

Elizabeth helped herself to a bottle of water closing the panel. Jani walked over to the screen as the bathroom door closed and tapped it. The aquarium disappeared replaced with a coded menu. She touched the screen again.

"This is a circular building. The elevator is in the centre and rotates if you want a different room at the same level. There are four levels and we are on level 2."

Up came a three dimensional layout of the complex with little to indicate what the various areas contained. She slid her finger across the screen and the image obligingly swung on its axis. Elizabeth had finished eating and was removing the crumbs from the corner of her mouth.

"You are free to go wherever you please though there are some areas that are off limits. I will return in an hour to take you to level one." She said pointing at the image. There is a projected holograph in the elevator and all you have to do is touch the area you wish to go to. I would like you to know that you are welcome here and if there is anything you want, please just ask."

SIS chief Sir Anthony Hollinger and Dame Amelia Sharp the Director of GCHQ accompanied by assistants stood in front of a large wall screen showing a number of real time satellite and drone images. "Was there anything useful on Doctor Graham's phone Amelia?"

"No nothing. Her contact list hasn't thrown up any leads. She doesn't have a particularly wide circle of friends and hardly any colleagues listed. Texts are mostly to her mother, her cousin in Inverness, a friend in Rapid City, South Dakota, Professor Stanford, just the usual kind of texts, nothing untoward."

"He has an idea where Doctor Graham is, I'm sure of it. Did he take the laptop?" Hollinger said.

"Yes he has. He might not be sure where she is but I believe he's got more of a lead than we have. There's a GPS chip in the case giving us continual position tracking to within eighteen inches. The solid state hard drive has been replaced so that the opposition cannot benefit from the original and it's powered by a hidden battery within the case, the battery compartment itself is filled with undetectable explosives that are perfectly safe. When the image recognition software camera sees Graham, a senior intelligence officer will be given the green to arm the detonator and the second she touches any key on the keyboard, end of problem."

"Where is he now?"

Sharp turned to the screen. "His taxi is heading for Heathrow. He's booked on an AirScotia flight to Glasgow. I don't understand his amateur cloak and dagger antics since he was once employed by SIS even if it was some time ago.

This pretence at holidaying in Scotland while holding tickets for a flight to Dublin and then onward to Vancouver is odd."

"Why Vancouver?" said Hollinger.

"I don't know."

"What do you think his plan is?"

"Well judging by the texts on her phone there is an emotional relationship between the two, could be serious, who knows. He may feel that he has a bargaining counter by possessing Elizabeth's laptop maybe doing a deal but, and this is a big but, He could be wrong. I think he has an idea but that's all it is. Wherever he's heading to it could be a wild goose chase down a blind alley," she said. "His background..." Amelia Sharp studied her notes. "...Born and educated in Exeter did his graduate and postgraduate degrees in the University of Exeter. He did his thesis on 'The correlation and effects of hormonal output in relation to cognitive ability in teenagers' His mother died in a boating accident off the north coast of Devon and his father is in a nursing home in Totnes suffering from Alzheimer's. He worked for us as a neurologist in psyops support for a year. He is thirty-eight years old possesses a clean driving license and of course a passport. He was married seven years ago to a Rhona Macbeth who was a court stenographer from Edinburgh. They are separated with no children. His medical records show nothing of any note as does his dental records."

"What about his online activities?"

"Our database scanning logarithms from his Google searches over the last five years have given us this profile. He is heterosexual, apolitical with interests in vintage cars, Thai cooking, Pre-Raphaelite art, and East-European and Californian wines. Payment activity provided by his bank reveals that there is only normal day to day use. His standing order and direct debits are mostly used for paying utility companies indicating that he is not a member of a club or organisation. He is not listed on Amazon, eBay or PayPal. He does not use any virtual private networks to mask his online surfing. We know this because logarithms show there are no comparison internet search patterns on the web or the dark web. His emails are exceedingly dull being mostly esoteric academia from scientists in various parts of the world. He has no sporting interests. His musical inclinations lie somewhere between Bach and the Beetles. He is not listed on any social media networking sites, Twitter, Facebook, or LinkedIn. We cannot track where he has been using GPS because he is using an IOS operating system with location services turned off. A list of calls from his mobile provider shows very little activity, hardly any actually. Isn't that rather strange? No texts at all and no web searches with only seven calls made in the last quarter to taxi firms and a care home in Totnes, very strange. The Stingray operator won't be able to locate his International Mobile Subscriber Identity ("IMSI") numbers and Electronic Serial Number in Canada. The Canadian authorities won't allow it. Mobile mast triangulation tracking records from his network provider however show that his movements over the past year are repetitive and predictable with a 5 to 10% variable. In other words, he's either a rather dull Mister clean or he doesn't like being tracked."

"Hi can I have a phone card and a copy of the Glasgow Evening Scot please?"

The woman at the till of the airport shop gave him a nice smile. "Ten or twenty?" She Asked.

"Oh ten pounds thanks." He received the card, the paper and the change and went in search of a payphone. Daniel dialled a number and it quickly rang out. He waited impatiently. "Come on, come... on."

The phone clicked and a male voice said "Hello?"

Daniel heaved a sigh. "Ian."

"Danny boy heavens how the devil are you?" asked Dr Ian Smith.

"It's good to hear you Ian. I'm coming to Canada. I don't want to say too much over the phone but I very much need your help. I'm at Glasgow airport right now and I'm just about to catch my flight to Dublin then a connecting flight to Vancouver."

"Wow, that's great but." Ian hesitated "What's up? It sounds like you're in a spot of bother."

"I've a lot to tell you. Do you still have that crazy Kolb aircraft?"

"Yes I do pal it's all boxed up in my garage."

"Ah, what kind of range does it have?"

"Not much, headwind maybe forty, tail wind maybe sixty miles."

"Oh" said Dan disappointed. "Could you meet me at the airport in Vancouver?"

"Of course, what time does your flight get in?

"Well it leaves Dublin 00.50 and it takes about nine and half hours. It's a little early, just after five in the morning is that Ok?"

"Sure."

How's Alice?"

"Oh just great, we have a boy now, Joshua he's nearly three. Do you ever hear from Rhona?"

"I only see her when she wants something which to be fair isn't very often. But I'm fine with that and she's happier, living with the orthodontist."

"Who?"

"Don't get me started. I'd better go and catch my flight."

"Ok, travel safe."

The Prime Minister was giving a statement at an emergency evening recall for Parliament. The Speaker of the House of Commons stood up. "The Prime Minister."

"I would like to thank you Mr Speaker and Members for returning to the House at such short notice.

I know I speak for all sides of the house in condemning this shocking terrorist act and our thoughts and prayers go to the families of those brave policemen and women who were killed while in the line of duty in cold blood and without mercy. Acts of cowardly violence will not stop our cherished values of democracy. Let me give a clear message to those responsible, we will find you and we will seek justice for this atrocity. I can assure the house that every possible avenue and resource will be channelled into bringing those responsible to feel the full weight of British justice. There are many here that do not share my views on many things but we will unite to defeat this evil."

"Hear! Hear! Hear!"

"Leader of the opposition."

"Hear! Hear! Hear!"

"Thank you Mr Speaker. I join with the Prime Minister in condemning this atrocity and our thoughts on this side of the house go with the families and friends of the victims. Does the Prime Minister agree with me that this terrorist attack in London on our serving officers present a threat to our democracy and national security unprecedented in modern times? And will the Prime Minister assure the house that the security services are in full control of the security of the United Kingdom. Further, will the prime Minister launch an inquiry into the failings of our security services in preventing this attack?"

"Mr Speaker I thank the Right Honourable member and welcome his comments. I have already ordered an inquiry because I believe that for the security of the nation there are lessons to be learnt and I will give this house a guarantee. I will not rest until the people responsible for this horrible crime are hunted down and brought to justice."

"Agent Ross, I can't keep calling you that, what's your first name." Mrs Ruby Graham was sitting on a swing on a porch in the heart of Yosemite National Park. She looked at him. His receding hairline had persuaded him in a fit of pique to shave it all off, and he liked it. He was small and well-built probably more to working out than too many burgers.

"It's Brian." He almost apologised for the name.

"Well Brian we're in God's own country, have you ever seen anything so beautiful?"

It was a simple two bedroomed log cabin with a large living room. A big natural stone fireplace had a log fire burning away and a wood stove for cooking. The air was tinged with pine wood smoke. They were surrounded by Giant Sequoia forests, massive mountains capped with plutons, geologist jargon for volcanic plugs and dotted around, the occasional deep green blue lake. Life here was as simple as it gets. Fresh water springs, no electricity, no radio, no internet, no mobile masts. Brian had a satellite phone in case of an emergency.

"Have you ever been to Scotland?" Brian shook his head. "It's like Canada in miniature. Apart from the Highland clearances that's probably why a lot of Scots settled there and that's where I met Elizabeth's father George." Ruby breathed in the scented pine and the wood smoke. "He was a private jet interior designer mostly for billionaires, though the airlines sometimes called him in as well. He was invited to Ottawa to give an after dinner speech. We lived there at the time and my father insisted that we all went to this dinner. I wasn't pleased because my friend was having a party that night. Well George stood up and started to speak and I was hooked. He was good looking sure and I knew a lot of good looking guys but he weaved a magic spell with his voice. George was raised in Fort William and educated in Aberdeen, a perfect blend of East and West accents. He told this story about a famous snooker player who wanted to practise on long haul flight. So he asked George if he could build a full size snooker table in his plane, a snooker table would you believe. After George got over his surprise he thought about it and set out to see if there was some way to make it work. So he designed a computer model with a very clever system of self-levelling weights and levers couple with anti-vibration dampers which was all theoretical of course not having been done before. Once he was satisfied he called the snooker player and told him he was ready to put it into practice. The snooker player was astonished and said he had been joking. Anyway after dinner I insisted my father introduce us and that was that. It was a whirlwind romance. He stayed on in Canada for a few weeks and then he had to go back to Scotland. Before he left he proposed then sang a song from Robert Burns that I will never forget."

'As fair art thou, my bonnie lass,
So deep in love am I;
And I will love thee still, my dear,
Till a' the seas gang dry.
And fare-thee-well, my only Love!
And fare-thee-well, a while!
And I will come again, my Love,
Tho' 'twere ten thousand mile!'

Ruby looked away. "Elizabeth's got her fathers red hair. Is there any way I can speak to her, can you at least tell me what's happening and if she's safe?"

"Ruby, I like you and if there was any way that I could help you I would. But I don't know anything because I'm not told anything. My job is to make sure you are safe. However I have the authority to disclose that I am in possession of a substance that might be of interest to you."

Brian Ross thought for a second searching his pockets. Then took out a joint putting it to his lips and set it alight with a zippo. He handed it to Ruby. The clear evening air began to turn a little blue.

"The last time I had one of these was at Woodstock." She looked at Brian. "Heard of Woodstock?"

Brian nodded and chuckled. "Of course I have, everybody's heard of Woodstock."

"I was a friend of Max Yasgur. He invited me to three days of peace music and love at the Catskills or as its better known of course, Woodstock in August 1969. There were 400,000 people there, can you imagine it, 400,000 people. Joni Mitchell, Crosby Stills & Nash, Bob Dillon, Arlo Guthrie, Joan Baez, Janis Joplin, the Who, Joe Cocker and on and on and on." She paused taking a drag from the joint. "And then there was Jimmy Hendrix." Ruby exhaled creating a perfect smoke ring. "Oh my, oh my."

The jet's tyres screeched as it landed wakening Daniel, a pale glow lit his face from the rising sun. "Ladies and gentlemen welcome to Vancouver Island. Local time is 5.44am and the temperature is nine degrees Celsius. Cellular phones may only be used once the fasten seat belt sign has been turned off." Daniel took out his mobile and slipped it under his seat where the life vests get stowed. "Please ensure you have all your personal belongings. We hope you have had a pleasant flight and on behalf of AirScotia Airlines and the entire crew, I'd like to thank you for joining us on this trip and look forward to seeing you again in the near future."

Sir Anthony Hollinger was watching a live four second delay image coming through from NSA's Menwith Hill satellite communications centre in North Yorkshire. The image beamed from the low altitude KH-11 HawkSat was using the latest Evolved Enhanced CRYSTAL telescope. This advanced satellite was also capable of tracking aircraft designed for Stealth Technology by analysing a logarithmic pattern of air disturbance caused by the aircraft. It showed in amazing clarity passengers disembarking from a jet at Vancouver Airport. With the ability to resolve objects six inches across coupled with face recognition processing, it was a formidable tool. Professor Daniel Stanford appeared at the door and a red square formed on his face and then turned green locking the image. An extraordinary amount of detail about location, time and date, weather and so on scrolled along the bottom of the frame. The camera followed him as he boarded an airport coach that headed towards the main terminal. 'Fishing in Scotland? Really professor, this may be a fishing expedition but not for salmon.' He thought. Amelia Sharp was shown into his office by George.

Queues started building up at immigration. There didn't seem to be many officers manning the desks. There were exhausted mothers with tired crying babies, well-dressed business men travelling alone, a girl's hockey team, all waiting for their turn and then Daniel. The lady immigration officer looked carefully at him before taking his passport. "Purpose of visit?" she asked scanning it.

"Tourism." He had learned not to get into a conversation of any length with immigration or customs.

She looked at her screen and back at Daniel then thumbed through the pages. Daniel was holding his breath and trying to look casually uninterested.

"Have a nice vacation professor," she said stamping his passport.

His rucksack was one of the last to come off the conveyor. He hooked it over his shoulder and walked through customs without being challenged. Waiting outside with a big grin was Doctor Ian Smith, sporting a dark brown beard and curly hair. They hugged each other slightly self-consciously.

The camera locked on to Daniel as he emerged from the terminal. He approached a man standing on the side-walk with his hands in his pockets. "Amelia do we have an active laser microphone embedded in HawkSat?"

"Yes but they're still having issues with it but what we do have is the latest lip reading software fresh out of the box. We can try synchronizing the two. It might give us an enhanced audio." She pressed a few buttons on her tablet and a digitized voice started up.

Ian whistled. "You look rough, come on." He took Daniel's rucksack.

"Me? I don't travel well and what's with the face fungus?"

Ian laughed "Got fed up seeing my naked face looking back at me. Vehicle's over here." There was a click and the boot opened. Ian put the rucksack in while Daniel got in the passenger seat. The screen went blank.

"Damn," said Hollinger. "What happened?"

"I believe they must be realigning the satellite. It has a very low geostationary orbit and the drag of the atmosphere means they have to fire boosters to increase the altitude. While they do that HawkSat goes offline."

The N10 north bound traffic was busy. Daniel looked out of the window. "Elizabeth's been kidnapped."

"Why would anyone want to kidnap Elizabeth?"

"She was working on something important and now she's gone. That maybe had something to do with it."

"What was so important that somebody would kidnap her?"

"I can't tell you that Ian, sorry." As the car headed towards Ian's home in North Vancouver, Daniel related the extraordinary happenings of the last twenty-four hours. "Remember Kamchatka, what a place all those Volcanoes and hot springs."

Ian nodded "And don't forget the grizzly bears, never seen so many before nor since."

"Is Petropavlovsk still like Dodge City? Run by the Russian mafia I remember."

Ian shook his head, "Haven't been there for a few years but from what I hear things have calmed down quite a bit." He pulled up outside a nice detached and painted timber built house. They were met on the porch by Ian's wife and young son. "Hey, this is Alice and this is Joshua, He's getting a big boy now, aren't you Josh?" he asked picking up his son. "This is an old friend of mine Daniel Stanford."

"Josh has always wakened early, haven't you Josh? You must be hungry come and have some breakfast," said Alice.

"Thank you," said Dan.

After breakfast Ian tapped Dan on the shoulder and winked. "Want to see my pride and joy, the other woman in my life and by coincidence she's also called Alice." They walked to the edge of a wood where there was a half-hidden boat house. Inside was Alice, a large powerboat. They clambered on board and went into the main cabin.

"I'm very impressed, what's its range? Could it reach Kamchatka?"

"No. Kamchatka's thousands of miles away. Full up and with lots of barrels stored onboard maybe 500 miles max." He looked at Dan.

Daniel frowned. "Whoever is behind Elizabeth's abduction has a great many talents. Creating synchronised semi-autonomous armed drones? Hacking ability superior to that of governments? So who do I know that's experienced in the dark web, robotics, electronics, advanced processors, artificial intelligence, neurology, graphene engineering, Nano-technology."

Ian whistled. Daniel nodded. "Yes that's who I think it is, Karl Orlov."

"But he died in a hot air ballooning accident over the Serengeti."

"I had a look at one of the drones used in the attack. On the tip of a rotor I could just make out an etched image of an eagle. Dr Karl Orlov aka the eagle was supposedly dead in the Serengeti. Yes but his body was so badly burnt that they couldn't get any DNA and he was headless. They thought hyenas had disturbed the remains."

"Convenient if you want to disappear. You two didn't get on as I remember."

"He didn't get on with anybody even with people he liked."

"You mean Elizabeth."

Daniel looked at Ian and smiled. "Even before he was a post grad. He was an arrogant so and so, absolutely brilliant of course, a genius really and at the same time incredibly stupid. How can that be Ian?"

Ian shook his head. "Dunno. Why are you so interested Kamchatka?"

"It's a bit of a wild guess. Conon Doyle once wrote, *Eliminate all other factors, and the remaining one must be the truth*. Orlov's cousin owned a large chunk of land including a lake close to the southern tip of the peninsula. How he managed that I don't know. It's supposed to be a wildlife reserve. Ian, how do I get there?"

"This is not a James Bond film and with respect you are not exactly built like James Bond. What are you going to do, smash down the door shoot your way past the guards sling Elizabeth over your shoulder while killing the baddie and as you both leave the whole complex explodes. In real life heroes can get killed. So if you're not going to do that, what? Knock on the door and say please may I have my girlfriend back?"

"Something like that, I could be completely wrong about all of this but I have to try and incidentally don't think you're going to be my back up buddy. You have responsibilities."

"Have you forgotten about the armed drones and in any case why would he kidnap Elizabeth?"

"I'm afraid I can't tell you that Ian, sorry."

"I've been offered a year's contract in Scotland with SAMS you know Scottish Association for Marine Science. It's on the West coast," said Ian.

"Oh, I was hoping you could help me out."

"Well I can they're very flexible. The project starts when I arrive basically." A silence descended. "I have a friend on Adak Island half way between the US mainland and Russia. I happen to know there's a regular cargo run from Anchorage. It takes about three hours. My friend Maxim, a Russian who was run out of Kamchatka by the mafia has a seaplane. I take it you don't want to go through the niceties of passport control and customs."

"Would your crazy lawnmower powered thingy fit inside the seaplane?"

Ian laughed. "Don't be rude about my Kolb and yes it would, just."

"Sounds good to me."

It was overcast with a leaden sky above the headquarters of the SVR. It looked like an anonymous office block in the shape of two Y's joined together with a high perimeter fence surrounded by trees in the Yasenevo District of Moscow. "Neurological Research Centre in London, why is that familiar to me?" SVR Chief, General Vladislav Golovanov was scanning the morning papers and talking to General Anatoly Grekov the Director of the Federal Security Service. (FSB)

"We had a sleeper there. His name escapes me," said Grekov.

"I remember," said Golovanov sitting upright in his chair. "Orlov, Karl Orlov isn't that a coincidence? We invested a lot of money in Doctor Orlov and we never did get anything worthwhile from him. Shortly after he was embedded in the NRC strange things started happening, files on the latest military satellite stolen, large amounts of Roubles being transferred from the Moskovskii Oblastinoi Bank...just a moment,"

Golovanov pressed a button on his intercom. "Demidov can you bring me the Karl Orlov file?"

Grekov continued. "We suspected Orlov but at the time we thought he was too valuable a sleeper to be pulled in for questioning. I believe he also received a substantial amount of money for his research projects from a number of Moscow, shall we say, business men who would very much like to meet him. There was a great deal of disappointment on his timely death," said Grekov.

Demidov came in with the file and put it on the General's desk. "Thank you Grekov this is most interesting."

4

*'There are over 5 million people in
America with security clearance.'*

A flashing icon appeared at the corner of Hollinger's tablet. He tapped on it revealing his secretary.

"Sir, Dame Amelia Sharp is here to see you."

"Thanks George." Hollinger made for the door and opened it. "Morning Amelia, come in."

Sharp tapped at her tablet. "Stanford's mobile is doing a regular run between Vancouver and London and he's stopped using his debit card so he's a little more street-wise than he wants us to believe. Now we only have HawkSat when it's ready and the laptop left to monitor his movements. Assuming he still has it, he's in a residential suburb in North Vancouver. The owner of the house is Doctor Ian Gerard Smith, forty-three year old marine biologist, married with a son. He is not known to us. We've checked his phone records and he took a call from a payphone at the airport shortly after Stanford's flight landed in Glasgow. North-west Telecom in Canada is not allowed to monitor the content of calls."

Sharp linked her tablet to Hollinger's monitor and started rotating an image.

"This is a street-view image of Smith's house. We are not allowed to use Optic-drones without special authorization in Canada."

Hollinger leaned forward and peered at the image. "Last thing we need are the Mounties gate crashing the party."

"There appears to be a boat house and a boat trailer at the bottom of the garden. Nice place right next to the water."

Hollinger nodded. "Perhaps there is an island or a coastal location Stanford wants to get to. If he's decided to go on holiday, why tell people he's going to Scotland, why the subterfuge? He's on to something and his friend is going to help. Run an in depth background check on Smith, we need to know what he knows."

"It's not going to be easy without involving the CIA and I doubt whether they could help us much anyway. The North Americans and Canadians are touchy about such things."

"What is Langley doing about all of this they've been very quiet considering they lost two agents?"

"They have been asking us all manner of questions. But we are in daily contact with the National Security Agency (NSA) and they have agreed to leave us to get on with it. There is an issue that we will have to address at PM level. In the longer term assuming we get Dr Graham back in one piece, the big question is do we let the Americans have a copy of Remembrance?"

"I'll set an appointment with the Cabinet Secretary. Anyway Smith is the key to finding out what our professor is up to. There must be some mutual link that could give us a clue. Ok Amelia, do what you can, thanks."

Sharp smiled. "My best analysts are running checks as we speak. It doesn't help having a name like Smith."

General Vladislav Golovanov was chewing a fingernail as he leafed through the file. Doctor Karl Orlov an ethnic Ingush born and educated in Minsk the only surviving child of Sergei and Katrina Orlov his two brothers having been killed in Afghanistan. Studied at the Belarusian State University in Minsk for his degree in robotic engineering and advanced quantum computer architecture. Recruited by the SVR and trained in hacking, spy satellite technology and counter insurgency. Enrolled at the NRC and delivered a thesis on Dynamical Computation, unravelling the mathematical principles behind intelligence, gaining his PhD. "How did you manage to do that and the other projects financed by the Russian mafia as well, extraordinary," he said out loud. "You certainly like to live dangerously even we couldn't protect you from them. Accident or not if it hadn't been for your little mishap you would have been in tiny pieces floating down the Moskva River being eaten by gulls. So far so good what about your personal life let's see." Golovanov read through the lists. Preferences, women, quite a lot of women by the looks of it, music, Igor Stravinsky, picked up a few medals in downhill skiing, loves poker and fishing. Psychological profile assessed by Doctor Mikhail Alexeyev. Karl Orlov has an IQ of 170. NB *It is possible for someone of his intelligence to manipulate psychological tests.* Nevertheless I have concluded that he is a paranoid schizophrenic with a multiple personality syndrome bordering on the psychotic, scoring ten out of a maximum twelve on the Schizophrenia Test and Early Psychosis Indicator. He has an ability to individually compartmentalize his feelings effectively separating them. The result is a psychologically complex individual on many levels who can be recklessly impulsive and meticulously precise, charismatic and abhorrent, kind and pitiless. The contrasts are only a hair trigger away. I am not his doctor but I would recommend an immediate course of chlorpromazine taken orally. "Charming, so Doctor Orlov you are back in circulation again," said Golovanov.

The door of the bathroom slid open opened revealing an almost clinical toilet and shower. Elizabeth walked in. There was a toothbrush and toothpaste, flannel, soap and shampoo. She had a sinking feeling that whatever the plan was she could be here for a long time. Elizabeth showered and dressed. She viewed her reflection in the mirror and ran a comb through her hair. Strangely despite the uncertainty of her circumstances, she saw a relaxed more confident Elizabeth than she had been for a while. The door of the elevator slid open and Jani stepped into the room. "Ready? Let's go."

They got into the elevator. Jani touched the hologram and the elevator ascended. The door opened. Daylight shining through a wall of glass hurt her eyes momentarily blinding her. She looked round the room and on one side a large screen fixed to the wall behind a polished steel and glass desk with the same tropical fish aquarium image. At the other side, a white rug on a polished wooden floor below a matching oval coffee table with four white leather chairs. Jani followed her in and leaned against a desk with her arms folded and a smile on her face.

"Ah Elizabeth, you're looking well." A male voice behind made her jump. She turned but there was no one there.

"Karl?" she asked, startled. "Karl Orlov?

"Who else," he said.

A man in his forties wearing a white shirt and white trousers with matching shoes slowly appeared as if from thin air. Round his waist was a large belt. His bald head was covered in tattooed hair and he sported a moustache. Elizabeth was in shock and could only stand with her mouth open. "But I thought you died in Africa and how did you manage to just appear?"

Orlov unclipped the belt covered in lenses. "I am very much alive and this is my latest toy," he said holding it up. "These lenses are connected to an 8k resolution camera system that converts and projects the images of a 3D hologram. The images you saw were recorded from behind and projected in front rendering any three dimensional subject completely invisible from all angles. I'm being rude. You've met before but never been properly introduced. Dr Elizabeth Graham this is my very good friend Jani Dhahabu. Her name means golden leaf in Swahili isn't that delightful? She is a very special lady very beautiful of course but she has a secret. Jani is from the Masai tribe in Tanzania, she and a guide were with me in the hot air balloon. She saved my life, pulled me from all that burning material and got badly burnt herself. The guide wasn't so lucky. I got off lightly. The villagers looked after us and I recovered but Jani had a weakened immune system and as a result she became infected with gangrene. We travelled to the nearest bush hospital in Tanzania but her arms and legs had to be removed to save her life. I took her with me and promised I would restore her limbs. She is wearing an exoskeleton that she controls using her brain without even the need to think about it. Jani is an engineering marvel her 'skin' is made from a special type of flexing piezoelectric material that produces a voltage when stress is applied and dynamically alters the molecules causing it to harden temporarily. The amount of hardening responds to the level of stress so much so that it can stop an armour piercing round. Forgive my bad manners," he said walking over to a chrome and black box on a table. "What would you like to drink?"

"You kidnapped me that was despicable?" said Elizabeth sharply.

Orlov laughed and bellowed. "You should be flattered it took a great deal of planning to get you here. Jani would you like something to drink?" She shook her head. "How about some lap sang souchong?" He said absent mindedly.

He prodded the touch screen on top of the box opened the 3d printer and put two cups with saucers in. The printer buzzed for a moment and then pinged. He took out the drinks beckoned to Elizabeth to sit and put the cups on the table but Elizabeth stayed where she was with her back against the glass wall arms folded.

"Elizabeth you are even more beautiful than I remember. With your long red hair you could have modelled for Rossetti. Rossetti? Dante Gabriel Rossetti? I believe Daniel is a keen follower of the brotherhood which explains his obsession with you." Orlov pointed at Jani. "Before I met you Jani, I had a soft spot for Elizabeth. But I knew I couldn't compete with the mighty Daniel. Ah Daniel, did you know that he was thrown into a pit full of lions for praying to God. An angel was sent by God to sew up the lips of the lions and the King made him free. Could always get out of a tight spot could Daniel."

Suddenly there was a sharp deep bell-like bong resonating from the glass wall behind Elizabeth. She turned to the window and screamed. A huge male grizzly bear was standing on his hind legs dwarfing Elizabeth with massive paws and long dirty claws touching the glass. Karl swivelled his chair round.

"Oh that's Boris. He's very nosy."

Elizabeth jumped as Boris slammed the glass with the flat of his paw again, yellow teeth showing as he growled. He went down on all fours and touched the window with its nose misting the glass.

"He seems to like you Elizabeth. I make a point of not feeding bears and then they don't associate me with food but nevertheless I'm glad I'm on this side of the glass with him around. Eh Boris, would you like to eat Elizabeth? I think so. By the way you're on the East coast of Russia, Kamchatka. A peninsula created by a string of volcanoes, some of them still active and home, as you can see, to the wild grizzly bear. There must be thousands. If you're thinking of going for a stroll by the way, I wouldn't advise it." Boris wandered off into the forest. "You are my guest. You are free to explore my home. There are one or two areas that are off limits but I think you'll find it interesting. You might find my lab I should say your lab is particularly fascinating. It is on the same level as your room. There are no stairs and no hallways every room is below us and connected by the elevator. If there is anything you need when you're outside of your room simple ask for Jani. You don't have to shout. You have your own voice respondent screen. There is a satellite connection for the screen in your room but I'm afraid you won't be able to access any news channels or the internet. I would suggest you get some rest because I have a lot to tell you and also there is much work to be done."

"You killed all these people."

"Yes I did," he said nodding his head.

"It was terrible."

"Yes it was," he said still nodding. "What a piece of choreography with those swarm-drones. They were made of a special polymer that self-destructs. They just disappear, another amazing invention from our friends in the US that I borrowed," he said. "I have a recording of the drones would you like to see it?"

"No, you're a murdering sick psychopath," she said.

Karl sighed. "No I don't think so. I don't like the sight of blood and under the circumstances, I had no choice. Killing should always be the last choice not the first, don't you think? Anyway, there are over a thousand military drones killing hundreds of people on a regular basis in the Yemen, Iraq, Afghanistan and Syria and probably Libya and that doesn't even include China's contribution. Don't tell me that's not murder."

"Don't you have any remorse?" she said.

"I never could afford that luxury. Elizabeth this is the real world, only the guiltless feel remorse."

"If you think for one minute I am going to work for, you you're not only sick you're stupid," said Elizabeth.

"Would you like to see your mother?"

"What! My mother is here?"

"Dear me no she's enjoying the sights of Yosemite with a friend."

Karl tapped the wristband projected hologram. 3d generated icons appeared around a screen suspended above his arm. He chose one and the huge screen that was an aquarium with exotic fish changed to an aerial image of a cabin in a forest. Karl made a circular motion around another icon and the camera zoomed in showing two people sitting on a porch.

"I have a circling high altitude Taranis drone. Taranis lovely word, it's called after the Celtic God of Thunder. The Americans manage to lose it during a trial, how careless. It is the very latest unmanned combat aerial vehicle (UCAV). Fully armed with laser guided missiles and it can stay aloft for another seven days. Well, I say Taranis but I have modified it so much that the name is no longer accurate. For example the fuselage is made of this wonderful graphene material making it very light and invisible to radar. Your mother is in the company of a CIA agent called Brian Ross who thinks he's a knight in shining armour. Charming isn't it. Elizabeth believe me, I have no wish to harm your mother. But you will work for me and we will start tomorrow."

"What do you want Karl, what is this all about?

"You are a small but important part of my grand design. I have a number of exciting projects. I'm going to save the world and you are going to save me."

The Prime Minister was busy in the cabinet office discussing the diary of the day with the Cabinet Secretary as Sharp and Hollinger entered. "Good to see you Anthony, Amelia please take a seat."

"Thank you Prime Minister," said Hollinger. "The Americans are making diplomatic noises about the Remembrance project. They want to know a bit more about its capability, how far the research went, how successful it was etc. And on the assumption that it works, an assurance that if all goes well with Dr Graham they would well, quite like access to it. I know there are a number of hurdles yet before we get there but it's important to think ahead."

The PM thought for a moment. "Well they are our allies however I don't think we should rush into things. Politically it could be an extremely sensitive issue if it were ever made public. The hoo-ha about rendition hasn't gone away and then Dr Graham might have something to say about it I'm sure. What do you two think Amelia?"

Sharp leaned forward a little. "In my view if Remembrance ever leaves our shores it is only a matter of time before it will spread. There are over 5 million people in America with security clearance, added to that they are still having problems securing Langley's servers."

"Gracious Anthony, How many people with security clearance do we have?"

"Well there are four levels of security clearance but we don't keep an official register of numbers in any of them. At a guess there must be, I don't know, tens of thousands. I agree with Amelia but the Americans are really not going to like it."

"I don't think it would be too difficult to sow some seeds of doubt about Remembrance," said the PM. "After all it is more than a little, fantastical, futuristic science fiction. There must be a sizeable majority of the five million security cleared personnel in America who would think that it's all tosh anyway."

The PM stood up and walked to the window, looking out at the rooftops and chimneys.

He sighed. "No. We'll just keep them in the dark for now. You know this must be one of the dreariest views in London."

Adak Island had no redeeming features. On 31 March 1997, the Navy closed Adak Naval Air Facility and from a high of 30,000 troops stationed here, only a few hundred maintenance staff remained.

"Ian this is a God forsaken place. Does it ever stop raining?"

He was standing at the entrance to a hanger that's roof leaked in places sending driblets of water onto the stone floor. Ian was busy with a claw hammer taking nails out of one of the panels of a box holding the Kolb.

"Yes it does," he said, "when it's snowing."

"Damn, how long are we going to be stuck here?"

"Don't know, Maxim says a day, two days maybe. The problem is getting the parts. This is a very old seaplane, older than I remember actually."

The two looked at the aircraft that was being dripped on. The hanger like the seaplane had clearly seen better days. Ian hammered the top panel up and removed it giving access to a side panel and an end panel which came off easily. They slid out the component parts of the Kolb and lined them up at the open door at the rear of the seaplane.

"Come on let's get these things loaded," said Ian.

Maxim jumped down from the plane's open engine cowling. "You should have called me earlier Ian. Once the parts arrive it'll maybe take about an hour to fit. My supplier is not very reliable though. Would you mind paying up front?" He shrugged wiping his hands on a rag. "I'm a bit short just now."

Daniel reached down and opened a flap on his rucksack and took out a bag with cash he got from Jill.

"British pounds Ok?"

The mechanic nodded. "I'll take anything, roubles, Yen."

"Here's five hundred, that's seven hundred and fifty dollars."

The mechanic took the money and slid it down the inside of his boot. "Can't be too careful around here, there's a lot of poor folk and empty bellies that need filling. So where are you heading to?"

"Dan is a photographer and he's desperate to get close ups of Giant Sea Otters. So we have one or two locations in mind."

"Haven't seen many of these round here you might have to go further west, maybe around the Attu Islands. Hey if you think this place is desolate just wait to you get there. The only people who go there are bearded birders. They go around in groups on bicycles looking for rare species."

It didn't take long between the three of them to load the separated Kolb fuselage and wings into the seaplane. The rain got heavier and the cloud base got lower.

Hollinger was annoyed. He didn't quite know why but that didn't change his mood. Maybe it was because the government was planning to move his staff out of the Vauxhall Cross building into the bowels of Whitehall. He was paid well enough at £169,999 a year but why they hadn't rounded it up for the sake of £1 he couldn't fathom. Yet it annoyed him that he hadn't had a pay rise for five years. His grown up son wasn't too demanding but his choice of girlfriends baffled Hollinger. His son had finished school and was planning a year out before going to the University of Winchester to study economics. He hadn't decided where. It was just another nagging worry for Hollinger. His wife Mary was loyal, dependable and knew him well. Her family lived in North Wales and occasionally she would sing a song in Welsh to Hollinger's irritation. The street lights lining the Thames came on. His thoughts were interrupted when Dame Amelia Sharp burst into his office. He wasn't amused.

"What is it Amelia?"

"Sorry Anthony your personal assistant George wasn't at his desk. The location signal from the laptop is stationary. Professor Stanford has travelled to the US owned Island called Adak. Now I have some information on Dr Ian Smith. He is a marine biologist and an old friend of Stanford. It seems they spent a lot of time in Kamchatka in Eastern Russia and Adak Island is half way between the US mainland and Russia."

"What was Stanford doing in Kamchatka?"

Sharp searched her file. "Apparently there was a family who all suffered from an extremely rare neurological disorder called Creutzfeldt Jakob Disease. It's a degenerative brain disorder and Stanford was researching how this cluster could have come about in one family for part of his thesis."

Sharp tapped her tablet and the screen on the wall flickered into life. "This is a view of the island from HawkSat. The image is very poor. The weather's not great so this is a composite from thermal and optical imagery. It is also noise reduced and enhanced although you wouldn't think it, and as you can just about see this is the airport with four hangers. The one at the top of the frame is where they are right now."

Hollinger joined Sharp near the screen. "Good work Amelia. Well we know where they are, and we think we know where they're going, but that's about it. Why would they be going to such a remote Russian peninsula? Do we have any audio monitoring?"

"No the conditions are not right for laser audio. We could have audio and video from the laptop but only if he opens the lid and switches it on. Then we will have a live feed."

"Do we have anyone in Petropavlovsk?" asked Hollinger.

"Yes we have two. They're Canadians working for us as helicopter maintenance engineers and they've been posted there to monitor airport traffic."

"Put them on standby, they could be useful."

Elizabeth left her room on level two and tapped the screen in the elevator. It didn't move, instead it rotated and the door opened. The room had a similar window monitor as Orlov's office on level one filling one side with same view. Apart from that it could have been her laboratory. On a table were familiar pieces of electronics, monitors and a large touch screen. It was almost as if all her things had been replicated. She powered up the computer and jumped back in surprise when a keyboard hologram suddenly projected from the base of the monitor. She typed her password into her login page and was astonished to find that she could feel the keys. The technology of superfast femtosecond laser pulses formed plasma voxels that made up the 3d image. It created the sensation of genuine keys when touched. She heard the door and turned round to see Karl emerge from the elevator.

"I don't understand. How did you manage to get all this here? You destroyed my lab. How could you possibly know about my equipment, and the programme?"

"So many questions so early in the morning," he said. "I had images relayed from the optic drone that was hovering outside the lab room window before it found you in the boardroom. The explosion was to ensure that you left the building quickly. But that doesn't matter what I want you to do is to refine and create a user friendly interface so that I can use your wonderful invention. With Remembrance there is a lot of unfinished business and loose ends that I can tie up. And also I have been trying unsuccessfully to hack into SIS servers for some time. I suspect they are using a very advanced form of security based on algorithms that monitor every user. Each person has a computer finger print, a unique way of typing, moving data about etc. etc. The second I enter and start working, it shuts down, very clever and very frustrating. It closes if there is any deviation from a user's profile. But SIS's friends in the CIA are not so smart. By the way SIS gave your files to the CIA."

"But how could they, my computer is not online."

"Breaking and entering is not my thing Elizabeth it's well, common thievery. No SIS broke into your lab and downloaded all the data onto an external SSD drive. They handed it over to the Americans. When I hacked into the CIA servers, I was just being nosy and I didn't want to leave a trail but then I saw Doctor Elizabeth Heather Graham's Remembrance folder. What a wonderful moment. I couldn't just take your file that would have been rather stupid so I transferred gigabytes of the stuff. It was a smokescreen. They wouldn't have known what I really wanted."

"I don't understand any of this."

"I'm working on a very advanced new form of computer technology but in the interim I'm using my own proprietary brand of quantum processors that can decrypt any level of encryption except quantum elliptical curve cryptography."

"How do you pay for all of this?"

"Pay, my dear girl I don't pay. Russian banks were kind enough to give me a loan, well maybe they wouldn't have done if they'd they had known about it. They have very poor security you know but now I have my own Bitcoin bank. I don't know the value of it I can't be bothered working it out. As I said SIS is almost the only organization I cannot hack. There is nothing I cannot do if I wished, utility companies, nuclear power stations, stock exchanges, police files, credit card companies, anything. But what you possess Elizabeth is unique, a much misused word. You have the power to read anyone's memory. Just think of the possibilities, they're mind blowing, if you pardon the pun."

"Decryption aside I wrote this computer model in such a way that only I understand how it works so they're all wasting their time," she said.

Orlov's studied her. "Precisely the reason you are here otherwise I would have completed it myself. One thing I don't understand. You are just a small step away from visualizing what the mind is thinking and yet you preferred concentrating on memory."

Elizabeth stopped for a moment in thought. "Scientists suggest that 98% of brain function is unconscious used for breathing, eating, beating heart, muscle use and so on. That leaves only 2% given over to involuntary and conscious thought. These are different levels of thought that meet and cross continuously. Involuntary thought is random haphazard volatile and unpredictable but all stemming from memory. So since most of the thoughts we have are random, teasing out conscious meaningful thoughts would be pointless and inconclusive. Who is to say that what a person is thinking is really what that person believes to be true. Or they might be thinking of something that never happened but that they'd merely like it to." Elizabeth stood up and walked over to the window. "This is an early version of Remembrance and it will take me some time to bring it up to date. I won't know how safe the memory erasure section of programming is to use until I do more extensive tests with a primate." She turned looking at Orlov. "The program needs refining. It could potentially be very dangerous possibly wiping the memory completely."

"You're far too modest Elizabeth I believe you are practically there. I want you to keep working on the software and the hardware to make sure it's all working or to make any changes if need be and, I've ordered a primate."

Lee Booker beckoned in Roy Pearson the Directorate of Analysis as he entered his office at the CIA headquarters at Langley chewing his unlit cigar. The last time he lit one of these was four years earlier just before having a mild stroke. There were no papers on his desk just a flat touchscreen. He hated this tech stuff but learned enough to get by.

"Roy, what's the latest on this missing American scientist?" He tapped his screen. "Doctor Elizabeth Graham. What are the Brits doing about it?"

Roy put his hands together. "I get the feeling that they want to go it alone on this one because they are not volunteering much Intel. We ask and they sparingly provide snippets. Maybe it's because they haven't got much to go on. I don't know, but they're barely keeping us in the loop. A funny thing though, they seem to be cooling on the veracity of Doctor Graham's research."

"You mean they're making out that's it no good?"

"Maybe, who knows?"

"Well the good Doctor may have the answer, and there's somebody else out there who believes it does work."

"Hang on Lee I'm getting something from the CSIS (Canadian Security Intelligence Service) in Ottawa routed through the NSA." Roy read the report coming in. "A Doctor Ian Smith and a Professor Stanford, that's Doctor Graham's boss has flown to Anchorage and then on to Adak Island."

"Where the hell is that?"

Ian took off despite a very low cloud base and skilfully piloted the seaplane low over the sea to avoid the radar. The time difference meant that they would arrive at Kamchatka at 16.30 hours after the three hour journey, exactly the same time they left Adak. They flew over a group of small Japanese fishing boats causing astonished faces that were clearly visible looking up. The sea was taking on an angry look whipped up by a strengthening wind. On the horizon the unmistakeable outline of Kamchatka's volcanoes were getting bigger.

"We can't land in the sea, it's too rough and the wind is coming from the south whipping up the water in the lakes but there's a relatively flat piece of snow as I remember high up inside one of the dormant volcano craters. We can try landing there."

"Try? Landing on snow with a seaplane? Inside a volcano?" asked Daniel.

Ian grinned. The seaplane increased height as they crossed the coast flying over a carpet of green, one colour of a many mosaics of tundra, forests and rivers of Kamchatka. Flying round the mountainous volcano steadily gaining height, the air turbulence increased and then Daniel saw the postage size patch of white snow.

"You've got to be kidding."

"It's a little smaller than I remember," Ian admitted. "But we should be Ok."

They flew over the rim and descended into the caldera. The stall warning alarm blared continuously adding to Daniel's discomfort. The air shielded from the incoming weather by the rim of the caldera was still. But they seemed to be going too fast. Ian was attempting to use the full length of the snow field. Daniel looked at him; the cheerfulness had gone replaced by grim concentration. The seaplane hit the snow and bounced accompanied by a loud bang. Ian immediately put the engine into reverse thrust and as soon as the hull hit the snow again the drag of the surface of deeper snow slowed the plane with only a few yards to the rising rim wall to spare. Ian slowed one of the engines and revved up the other turning the plane round causing the wing to scuff the rim wall. Satisfied he switched off the engines and the electronics.

"Whew, that was close."

He unfastened his harness folded his maps away and turned to look at Daniel who was as white as a sheet.

"Ian, don't you ever do that again."

"We're going to have to if we're ever going home buddy. Now that is going to be hairy," he said taking off his helmet. "Well chief we're here, what's the plan?"

"We'll unload the Kolb from the seaplane and start putting it all together, thank God it's sheltered, how long will it take?"

"Not very long it's mostly assembled really so we have to attach the wings, the rotor, the rubber apron and a few other bits and pieces. Let's get started."

Jani and Karl had been watching on the large wall screen as the seaplane landed on the snow in the volcano. The image had been viewed and relayed from a high altitude hovering optic-drone.

"It seems we have company. What a fascinating piece of airmanship. There are not many people who can do that. I believe I know who our uninvited guests are. Why would they want to land a seaplane on the snow in a volcano? How eccentric. We must invite them round for a drink. I think we may have Elizabeth's primate I ordered."

Lee Booker was pacing around his office holding a mobile.

"Roy what's our satellite capability in that part of the world?"

"It's well covered but there are severe weather restrictions in that area. Logically, if they continue their present direction it would take them into Soviet territory. The Soviets don't take kindly to satellites stationed above them. We've already lost a high value one. Should I put a request through to GCHQ?"

"No. You would think that they would have told us about this before now. There's no sense in letting them know what we know just yet."

An alert began flashing on one of a bank of sixteen computer monitors in a dimly lit room at GCHQ. A young woman coms officer punched on a record button and patched in a connection to the incoming signal. Daniel's face appeared.

"What are you doing?"

It was the voice of someone off camera.

"I'm going to try some passwords that Elizabeth might have used."

The officer picked up the phone and punched in a couple of numbers.

"Ma'am I have audio and visuals from the target laptop coming from the south of Kamchatka. I'm just patching it through to you now. Yes Ma'am Sir Anthony as well. According to the GPS, it appears to be inside a volcano."

Ian's face appeared behind Daniel. "Any luck?" he asked.

"No, I didn't think she would be quite so careful. I've tried her date of birth, her mother's maiden name, her pet's name, her car registration plate, absolutely nothing works."

"How come you know so much about Elizabeth?"

"Shut up and anyway what are you doing in here? You should be putting that flying lawnmower together."

"Did I ever tell you what this flying lawnmower can do?"

Daniel groaned.

"The Kolb Firestar seaplane has a cruising speed of 80 MPH, stalling speed of 27 MPH which means it's possible to hover in moderate winds. Take off distance with two of us is two hundred feet, One hundred with just one. It has a rubber apron that means we can land on the snow or on water or on the grassy tundra..."

"...Ok enough you sold it to me."

"It's finished," said Ian. "But the weather's looking really awful, I think we should hold off until first light because it's beginning to get dark now and I can't fly the Kolb in the dark, what do you say?"

"Ok. I'm getting nowhere with this contraption." Daniel turned off and closed the laptop. The screen went dark at GCHQ.

"You guys make me laugh." said Ian as he climbed fully clothed into a double sleeping bag. "I don't get it. How you two can't see that you were made for each other beats me. Why don't you just do the caveman thing, club her and drag her off by her hair to a cave somewhere?"

Daniel snorted. "Club Elizabeth, you must be joking she's bigger than me for a start and she'd probably kill me with the club."

"I don't mean literally, you wimp, take charge, tell her you're the boss. Stick up for your gender."

"I've tried that." Daniel's face flushed he was glad it was dark.

"Well, what happened?"

"She just laughed. She thought I was being funny. Anyway is that what you did to Alice?"

"Didn't need to my friend, Alice was besotted from day one. Why didn't you marry Elizabeth?"

"It's personal."

"Ok, just making conversation. I think it's going to be a long night."

There was an awkward silence.

Daniel sighed. "Did I ever tell you how I met Elizabeth?"

"No."

"I was passing Euston Railway Station and I saw a gorgeous woman with flaming red hair having an argument with a taxi driver. She was trying to pay him with Scottish notes and he wouldn't accept them so I paid. She was in a hurry so we exchanged mobile numbers. I saw her quite a lot while she was in London and then she had to go back to Aberdeen. And that was that until a couple of years later out of the blue she turned up at the NRC. I couldn't believe it. However by then, she was seeing someone. Soon after she broke it off, don't know why, and we started seeing each other again. Then I asked her to marry me and she said she wasn't ready for marriage. I took that as a brush off. I was stupid."

"You were stupid, I was lucky."

"There's a very strong sulphurous smell here. I hope we're not going to waken up dead tomorrow," said Daniel.

"I did a course on volcanology during my degree. If I remember correctly the gases emitted are mostly carbon dioxide and sulphur dioxide, but you also get carbon monoxide, hydrogen chloride, methane, hydrogen bromine and even mercury and a few other sulphides in much smaller amounts," said Ian.

"Thanks, that's given me piece of mind."

Daniel pulled the sleeping closer to his chin and yawned.

"Did you know that Wagner conducted Beethoven's symphonies from memory, you know without a score?"

"Dan I'm getting worried about you, have you ever thought about taking up a hobby?"

Daniel smiled. "Good night."

Even with double sleeping bags and the doors of the seaplane closed it was a bitterly cold night. Daniel lay there in the darkness listening as Ian's snoring started. He could sleep anywhere. Unwelcome questions filled his head. What if this was all a waste of time? What if Ian couldn't get the Kolb out of here?

What if Elizabeth was already de...? What if, what if. He turned over and dozed off.

"Where are the doors?"

Silhouetted against an early dawn sky, Daniel was leaning with one hand on the Kolb.

"Doors, what do you need doors for? It just adds weight. Get in."

Daniel threw his rucksack in the back and climbed in. They fastened their helmets and secured the full body harness's. The magneto fired up the engine first time much to Ian's delight and Dan's relief. He revved it up and let it tick over for a minute. Then finally revving the engine and with a thumbs up they shot forward sliding easily on the snow and cleared the rim of the volcanic caldera with ease. The air was crisp and still in the early morning light making the flight enjoyable. The spine of magnificent snow-capped volcanoes that made the Kamchatka peninsula disappeared to the North. The air temperature increased as they descended. Ian was showing off now, almost skimming the tops of the Stone Birch trees towards a river. Thousands of sockeye salmon were clearly visible in the shallows. Ian narrowly avoided flying through smoke-like, rising columns of millions of mosquitoes. The Kolb followed the meandering river skimming over the water and as they rounded a bend, a group of bears stood up then ran for cover into the forest. Beyond a flat piece of land and almost hidden in the forest was what appeared to be an odd looking circular single story building. Daniel pointed to an area of open tundra edging the forest and Ian nodded. The aircraft touched down as the grass hissed underneath the aircraft over a surprisingly short distance. Ian cut the engine.

"What now?" he said.

Daniel took off his helmet, unfastened his harness grabbed the rucksack from behind and stepped out of the aircraft.

"I want you to get the hell out of here, back to the seaplane and stay there. If this crazy thing works Elizabeth and I will join you. If you don't hear from us in two hours go home and leave the Kolb behind, you'll never get it and the seaplane out of that volcano anyway." They shook hands.

"Ruby wake up," Brian gently shook her shoulder.

"Is everything Ok?" asked Ruby yawning. "It's still early Brian," she said turning over.

"I've got a text, the boss is coming he wants to talk to you."

"Your boss?" asked Ruby.

"Yes my boss and everyone else's, Lee Booker the Director of the CIA. He's coming here."

Ruby sat up. Brian was already dressed wearing a dark suit white shirt and tie and he looked a little anxious. She got out of bed and headed for the shower. Brian looked at his watch for the third time in as many minutes. He went into the kitchen and made coffee and pancakes. Ruby appeared wearing a pale blue dress, kissed him on his shiny bald head and sat down. She poured herself some orange juice and looked at him.

"Why are you nervous? You look like you're going for a job interview."

Brian smiled. "Guys on my pay grade don't get to meet the boss."

He looked out of the window.

"They're here."

Four men got out of a car and walked up the steps of the cabin and waited at the porch. Brian opened the door went out and shook hands. Ruby stood up as they entered. Brian gestured.

"This is Mrs Graham, Mr Booker." They shook hands.

"Thanks Agent Ross." Brian looked at Ruby and left to join the others outside.

"How are they treating you Mrs Graham?"

"I'm being treated very well thank you. Please call me Ruby."

"And you can call me Lee. Ruby may I sit down?"

"Please. Would you like some coffee?"

"Yes please black and lots of sugar. I hope you don't mind this sudden intrusion Ruby you've probably guessed it's about your daughter. The British government are trying everything to find her and we have offered them any assistance they might need. Elizabeth has become a very important person because of her work and I'm here to see if you might be able to help." Lee took a sip of coffee. "Did Elizabeth have any enemies?"

"Not one."

"We've been going over all the scenarios and none of them fit to any pattern. Do you know what she was working on?"

"No I don't, sorry."

"Did you ever visit her at the Neurological Research Centre in London?"

"Yes I did once but it was quite a long time ago. My husband and I stayed with Elizabeth for Christmas. We were invited to the NRC Christmas party and then we planned to spend New Years' eve, I mean Hogmanay in Scotland."

Lee helped himself to a pancake. "These are delicious Ruby you are a very good cook. You see whoever took Elizabeth was convinced that she was working on something quite extraordinary and must have concluded that her project would work. I can't go into detail Ruby you understand but I have this feeling that Elizabeth knew her kidnapper. You know here in America 76% of kidnappers are known to their victims. Now for someone to understand the significance of what she was doing, meant that it had to be a person with a certain amount of knowledge on experimental neurology. It may have been a colleague."

"No, you're not suggesting her professor, Daniel Stanford, impossible."

"I'm not suggesting the professor but you see where I'm going with this?"

Ruby glanced at the window and saw Brian anxiously looking in.

"Were there many people at the party?"

"Not many, it's quite a small department. Let's see, well there was Elizabeth and Daniel and his assistant Jill, there was the technician, what's his name um Frank. There were about six or seven PhD students, I don't know their names and a couple of visiting professors, the Principle, can't remember his name either and there was a very handsome man Eastern European, no Russian who was slightly drunk. My husband didn't care for him much. I remember him because he insisted on introducing himself as the eagle so I can't help you with his name I'm afraid. I think that was it, oh the receptionist Harry or Henry something like that."

Lee absent mindedly helped himself to another pancake deep in thought. Ruby glanced at the window again but Brian wasn't there. Lee stood up and opened the outside door.

"Anybody here speak Russian?"

Brian put his hand up.

5

"O memory! thou midway world twixt earth and paradise,
Where things decayed and loved ones lost in dreamy shadows rise"
Abe Lincoln

The forest was dense, thick enough to hide a hundred grizzlies. Daniel was extremely anxious. Every step could take him face to face with an eight hundred pound bear. He stopped motionless listening intently. Behind him he could hear Ian taxiing and taking off. As the sound of the aircraft faded he felt horribly alone and vulnerable. He thought he heard something dead ahead. Frozen to the spot, he waited until a deep angry growl stung the air as a huge shadow ran crashing through the vegetation to his left. Daniel was shaking. Possibly if he hadn't stopped, he would have walked straight into the bear. He had been following a little trail. Was that wise? It was likely a bear track but he had no choice, he kept going. The thermal imaging optic-drone had followed him from the Kolb flying over the forest tracking his body heat. Eventually he emerged from the forest onto a strange patio leading to a semi-reflective glass wall. Daniel walked up and saw himself for the first time in a while. Stubble had grown on his face and it looked like he'd been camping for days. Karl and Jani watched from inside. Karl touched his Holoband and chose an icon that began sliding the door open.

"Daniel, my dear fellow, what took you so long? Come in, come in. Jani meet the very eminent Professor Daniel Stanford with a CBE now, I believe, congratulations."

Daniel took off his rucksack and looked around the room. "Hello Karl. I'm impressed. So this is where you've been hiding all these years. Of course it begs the question, whatever for?"

"Moja kwa moja Daniel one thing at a time, would you like some refreshment? Tea or coffee?" he said.

Daniel ignored the question. "What have you done to your head?"

"I'm afraid the intense heat from my ballooning adventure needed major plastic surgery and irreparably damaged my follicles. This is a tattoo do you like it?"

"Not particularly, you'll have to get grey hairs tattooed on it when you get older. Why did you disappear?"

"I made the best out of a bad situation and decided that dying would suit my purposes at the time, let's say that there were a number of gentlemen in Moscow who I owed favours to. Favours I couldn't pay back and anyway I'm enjoying being dead. Life is so less complicated. You should try it. Jani I wonder if you could ask Elizabeth to join us?" The outside door was sliding shut. "Can't be too careful, there are a lot of rather large bears I'd prefer not to meet out there but then you know that, you almost bumped into one in the forest. For a moment I thought you wouldn't be able to join the party. By the way that was a miraculous piece of flying landing the seaplane inside a volcano, can't think why you would need to. It was seriously awesome, a little foolhardy maybe but very impressive. Dr Smith I presume."

The elevator door slid open and Elizabeth appeared. She stopped and gasped putting her hand up to her mouth, then ran forward to embrace Daniel. They held each other. Daniel was pleased and a little surprised. Elizabeth rarely showed her true emotions.

"What are you doing here?" She said

Karl applauded sarcastically. "What a touching scene and a very good question."

Daniel ignored him. "Are you alright?"

"Yes, yes I'm fine, really I'm) Ok."

"I'm here to take Elizabeth home Karl."

"My dear fellow, you've only just arrived and Elizabeth is staying because she has agreed to work for me for a short while."

Daniel looked at Elizabeth. "He has an armed drone circling above the cabin in the Yosemite where my mother is."

Daniel moved towards Karl and stopped when Elizabeth's arm went out. Jani took up a position closer to Karl.

"I'm here to do a deal." said Daniel.

"What could you possibly have, that I would want?"

Daniel opened his rucksack and took out the laptop.

"Daniel!" she said, "where did you get it?"

"I demanded it back from SIS. Karl everything you need is here. You don't need Elizabeth."

"This is a very bad idea Dan, in fact it's the worst idea you've come up with. The very latest trials and updated data are all on there. Do you realize what would happen, what the consequences would be? In any case I'd still be the target for every crackpot half-baked regime in the world."

Dan put the laptop on the glass table and looked at Elizabeth.

"We could work something out, disappear." He turned to Karl. "What do you say?"

"Well I already have Elizabeth working for me so I don't really need the laptop but, it might save some time perhaps. Daniel you're not very good at this are you. You have no bargaining chip. But I have plans for you. Elizabeth is in need of a primate. You are my guest here until I say otherwise as is the fiery maiden." Karl sat down on a white leather chair. "I don't think you've been entirely open with Elizabeth about your past."

Daniel and Elizabeth sat down. "I'm not sure I quite understand what you mean." He said.

"Your CBE, was for services to the Secret Intelligence Service?"

Daniel noticed Elizabeth's surprise.

"Yes for a short while that ended some time ago."

"Let me see now weren't you an analyst at SIS?"

"No, psyops support and I was actually based at Chicksands in Bedfordshire with 15 Psychological Operations Group for a year but I was seconded to SIS for three months, why?"

"I want Elizabeth's help to jog your memory about something that is very important to me. It's a matter of pride more than anything else, unfinished business and then we're done, easy."

"You knew I would come here," said Daniel astonished, "but how? Of course the eagle on the drone, that was deliberate?"

"Yes of course and I hadn't forgotten your friend, Dr Smith, a very resourceful man. But it's good that you managed to see my little clue before it disappeared."

"How did you do that?"

"One of the folders I ahem retrieved from Langley contained details of an extremely interesting polymer material that self-destructs after use."

Elizabeth took Daniel's hand. "SIS is the only organization that Karl has not hacked."

"Once I am satisfied that I can make Remembrance work for me and I have what I need from you." He said pointing at Daniel. "You're both free to disappear or whatever you wish to do, I'll even help you. Of course I will have to delete some things from your collective memories before you go."

"You'll never get access to SIS servers, its' impossible." said Daniel. "The master passphrase is thirty-seven alpha-numeric characters long held in a secure safe. Two senior members of staff with separate keys open both locks of the safe and stay in your presence until you set up your user account, then the passphrase is locked in the safe again. I couldn't possibly remember that. In fact that's expressly why it's so long so that no-one can remember. No paper, no pencils, pens, phones or cameras allowed."

"I'm sure that Elizabeth's little box of tricks won't find that a problem. Once I have the master passphrase I will open a new user account. There will be no fingerprint for the security system to gauge or compare it to. I will have total access to SIS servers," he shrugged. "If it doesn't work, I'll try something else. Giving up is not something I ever do."

"I won't do it, it's too dangerous. If I make a mistake I could end up wiping Dan's memory completely. He could end up a vegetable."

Orlov laughed. "Elizabeth I have a great deal more faith in you than you have in yourself," Karl said slowly, the smile had gone. "None of us are in charge of our own destinies, not even me." He looked at them both and stood up. "It's settled." Orlov left the room.

Elizabeth put her head in her hands and pushed back her hair. "I need a date Dan. Can you remember exactly when you set up your user account? I want to spend as little time as possible poking around in your brain."

Dan thought for a while. "Oh, it was a week after the new millennium, 7th January 2000. Time was somewhere between ten and twelve o'clock in the morning."

"I'm much further on than Karl thinks. I don't really need this."

Elizabeth slid the laptop round and lifted the lid. She peered at the screen and was aware of the reflection of Jani watching from the door. She looked round at her as Jani turned and left.

At GCHQ, a flashing alert sounded from a computer screen. The analyst pressed record and saw Elizabeth's face. She picked up the phone.

"Ma'am we are at code red. The target has opened the laptop. Yes Ma'am. I'll arm the package and patch the image through"

She put the phone down glanced at the screen typed in a security code and pressed enter. A red line lighting the bezel of the screen started to pulse. The analyst watched as Elizabeth looked at her login page on the screen and her fingers poised over the keyboard. The background behind Elizabeth changed when she picked it up still looking at the login page. Then she closed the lid and the screen went blank.

"It's not mine." She whispered.

"What?" Said Daniel

"Of course it is. It's unmistakeable."

"Well yes it is mine I know but there's something wrong. The screen came up too fast, mine was always quite slow. It used to annoy me and the weight...this is definitely heavier. You say they just gave you the laptop?"

"Yes, well I was adamant."

"I don't understand," said Elizabeth putting her arms round Daniels waist.

"Don't worry; I'll get you out of this even if I have to use my bare hands to choke the life out of him"

"Don't be silly Daniel nobody's choking the life out of anybody."

The analyst picked up the phone again. "Did you see that Ma'am? I'm almost certain she's worked out that there's something different. No Ma'am I can't deactivate the package. Anyone who touches any keys now will send a current to the detonator"

"Why would they alter my laptop? What's different about it? Does SIS want to get rid of me?" Elizabeth frowned.

Daniel held her tight. "I don't know, maybe, I couldn't take the risk. That's why I had to find you; there was something the Director of the Secret Intelligence Service said at the COBRA meeting."

"The problem we face is that even without the laptop she may be able to re-create her work in another laboratory and that would be extremely dangerous and unacceptable, you understand? I cannot emphasize enough how catastrophic that would be."

"I am so sorry Elizabeth how could I have been so stupid? It must be a bomb. Wait, I tried putting in passwords when we were at the seaplane."

"What seaplane?"

"The seaplane we flew into the caldera."

"What caldera?" Elizabeth shook her head. "You're not making any sense now."

"Inside the volcano. Never mind that, I opened you're laptop and tried some words I thought you might use."

"Really, Like what."

"Well I started with your date of birth, then your car registration number, then I typed in pepper, then I tried p3pp3r."

"Elizabeth yelped. "You are clever and that was very close. I used her full name p3pp3rp0t, so maybe you were lucky you didn't get it."

"OK so what does that mean?" asked Daniel. "They probably have a GPS tracker so they'll know where we are and it's technically possible that they had hacked the microphone and the camera meaning that while the laptop was open they would have heard and seen everything. Logically they could have set a booby trap only it wasn't me they wanted it was you."

"Do you really think they would do that?"

Daniel nodded. "Yes I do and by the way GCHQ's MyNOC team, sorry that's My Network Operations Centre, broke into your flat and hacked the laptop containing all Remembrance research data. It wasn't me."

"I know," she said. "What a mess, how do we get out of this? We've got a Russian mad man on one side and a rogue secret intelligence service trying to hunt me down on the other."

Daniel let Elizabeth go, walked to the window and watched the glint of what could have been a seaplane taking off from the volcano.

"What is Orlov up to? It's not just about you is it?"

"He says he's going to save the world. He's quite mad you know," said Elizabeth. "I'm convinced that London knows where we are and I'm in no doubt that given half a chance they would blow us and Orlov to Kingdom come. What's worrying me more at the moment is this. What are they going to do next? They can't just bomb us. I think Russia would have something to say about that and as for getting out of here, we'll just have to do what Orlov wants and bide our time."

"What are our assets near Kamchatka, Murray?" The Prime minister was addressing a COBRA meeting at Whitehall.

Defence Minister Murray Greig looked at his papers. "We have a submarine about twelve hours from the coast of Kamchatka. It's well within missile range but any launch would be spotted by the Russians and immediately take us into full scale nuclear war. It's not possible to operate drones in Soviet territory it's far too politically sensitive. There are the two operatives in Petropavlovsk airport with access to a helicopter and that would be a three hour journey to get down to the South of the peninsula We've already lost an American satellite to Russia but we do have a nano laser burst capability from our military satellite once it gets into position in about seven hours. Again that would be highly sensitive and could invite retaliation from one of their weaponized satellites."

"Is that it?" asked the PM.

"It's a very remote part of the world sir."

"What about the SAS, can we parachute them in?"

"HMS Intrepid has an SAS reaction force four hundred miles away which when deployed could possibly be one hour thirty minutes to target location barring any reaction from the Soviet Air Force, and they are most likely to react. Although it's a remote part of Russia they have many listening posts on land and in space. They also have five Beriev A-50 airborne early warning and control (AEW) aircraft using the latest long range listening devices that has a tracking range of 230 Kilometres.

America has at least one satellite that is nuclear powered and is armed with a megawatt carbon dioxide laser utilizing a solid state infrared beam of energy but they won't give out any more information than that. They test fired it successfully at their Tonopah Test Range installation in Nevada. I don't know where the satellite is stationed. In fact even those holding the highest security are on a need to know basis. The Russians have Jarilo and Perun class laser satellites secretly developed and built after the failed Polyus-Skif laser satellite program. It had an expensive ending in space in 1987. They also have a soft hit capability. When they find a spy satellite it's knocked out of orbit just like the American one that was lost recently. The satellite burns up in the atmosphere giving the Russians plausible deniability. Jarilo has an anti-satellite and anti-intercontinental ballistic missile function but the Perun we're not so sure about. Given that they have ominously named it after the Slavic God of thunder and lightning there is speculation it could be used on terrestrial targets."

A buzzer sounded. Sir Anthony Hollinger looked at his mobile and pressed his touch screen several times.

"Excuse me Prime Minister I think you should see this."

He synchronized with the wall monitor. Elizabeth's pale spectacled face appeared.

"Oh my God," said Hollinger.

Elizabeth was staring straight at the camera, unblinking for a full ten seconds. Then she spoke slowly.

"I don't know if you can hear me but if you can my name is Doctor Elizabeth Graham. Professor Daniel Stanford and I are in the South of Kamchatka being held prisoner by Karl Orlov. Please help us."

"Can we communicate with her?" said the PM.

"No."

The screen faded to black. Hollinger did a quick internet search. "Karl Orlov apparently died in Africa some years ago. But that could explain a great many things that have happened in the banking sector and the American Dow Jones," said Hollinger.

The PM pointed at him. "Send an email to our ambassador in Moscow. Make sure the Russians can read it. Tell him that Orlov is alive and give his location and co-ordinates."

Brian came in and Ruby handed him a cup of coffee. "Well, very loosely eagle in Russian is Orlov."

Lee held out his hand to Brian. "Whatever you get paid Agent Ross it's not enough." He took out his mobile. "Hello, Roy do a search for Neurological Research Centre staff list in London going back ten years, I'm looking for someone called Orlov." Lee looked at them both. "You're quite a team you two."

"Would you like another pancake Lee?" asked Ruby. She didn't need to wait for a reply.

Lee's phone rang. It was Roy Pearson. "There was a scientist called Karl Orlov but it's looking like a no go. He was killed in an accident in Tanzania a few years ago. His hot air balloon went on fire."

"What about a body?"

"Badly burned, couldn't get any DNA."

"He's our guy. I want to know everything there is to know about him. Get our best analysts onto it and send an email to Hollinger in London. We may have found our hacker, Doctor Karl Orlov."

Hollinger was typing an email. "Langley's on the ball." He said wearily.

"Thanks Lee

We'll run a check on him, keep us in the loop.

Anthony"

"Lord this is just going to complicate things. They've found out its Orlov." He looked over to his deputy, William Thomson. "Bill what do the Russians know about Elizabeth Graham?"

"Cheltenham has been monitoring Russian chatter and there have been no references to her or to Stanford or Remembrance."

"Good, the PM wants us to send an email to the UK Ambassador in Moscow with the details of Orlov's location so use old encryption. The Russians might do our job for us."

6

"You'll have to fly."

"What! Are you crazy?"

"You fly or we die."

Elizabeth powered up the computer and the screen lit up immediately. The keyboard hologram appeared. It had taken a bit of getting used to but she quite liked it. She recognized the diagrams and various computer models from her original work that had been hacked by SIS and it hadn't been difficult for her to catch up. She brought up the latest active model that would be linked to the sensors. She would then 'talk' through the sensors to and from the neurotransmitters in the brain in a two way dialogue.

"This is a mild sedative that will make you very sleepy for a while." Elizabeth pushed a hypodermic needle into Daniel's vein. "But it won't knock you out."

Daniel lay on a couch with a number of sensors attached to his head. Elizabeth pulled out the needle and held a piece of cotton wool to stop the bleeding for a few seconds. Last minute calculations and everything seemed to be Ok. She looked at Daniel's closed eyes and regular breathing. The silent heart monitor on the screen showed a steady beat. She activated more programs. Using the computer model of the brain she guided the virtual probes to the hippocampus, entorhinal cortex and perirhinal cortex within the medial temporal lobe in order to interact with the declarative memory. At the top of the screen was a time date window showing the present. Elizabeth set it for 7th January 2000 and timed it for 0930. She took a deep breath and pressed enter. A deafening roar came from the wall screen followed by a piercing white light. Elizabeth turned the sound levels to almost zero and the noise turned out to be the interior of a car. Adjusting the video input levels from the computer to the monitor resulted in a clear image of the inside of a taxi.

"Wow I didn't think I could get you working again," she said.

"Of course it's working; I have absolute faith in you," Orlov said.

Elizabeth jumped in surprise; she was so engrossed she hadn't heard him come in. He stood there with a broad smile across his face.

"Congratulations Elizabeth, well done."

Elizabeth recognized that the taxi was travelling along Knightsbridge. She made a small adjustment to the time and the taxi stopped outside 85 Albert Embankment in Vauxhall. The unmistakeable architecture of the Vauxhall Cross building was the home of SIS. Daniel paid the driver and left the taxi. Elizabeth moved the time forward to 10.30 and Daniel was descending on an escalator towards, what looked like an underground tube station with desks randomly scattered round many large plain brick pillars arched at the top. He was met at the bottom by a young woman.

"Doctor Stanford, can I offer you a cup of coffee? Have you come a long way?

"No not far. I'd love a cup thanks."

Elizabeth moved the time on another twenty minutes and Daniel was on the move again following the same woman along a corridor until they entered a very plain office with a safe on one side of a desk supporting a computer terminal. Daniel had been followed in by a man. The two agents produced a key each and simultaneously opened their respective locks. The woman turned the handle and the door swung open. The man switched on the computer while the woman took out a small leather case, unzipped it and produced a laminated card with the master passphrase. Daniel leaned forward and read the passphrase.

"Stop the clock," said Orlov.

The image stopped and slowly began to fade. He punched a 3d icon on his Holovue catching a screen grab and filed it away in a folder before the screen went black.

"Thank you."

Elizabeth carefully stopped and closed the various apps and open windows on the computer screen. Orlov had gone leaving her alone with Daniel. She undid the sensors on Daniels head until they were all off. Elizabeth held his hand. It had been a triumph of sorts but it left her feeling deflated. She should have been screaming and jumping with joy, phoning her friends, submitting her paper to the Nature Neuroscience magazine but there was just emptiness as if something you really wanted all your life wasn't quite what you expected. Perhaps she had wasted all these years keeping Daniel at bay. He was still technically married, but so what?

"Dan." She said gently putting her hand on his stubbly face.

Daniel's eyes opened and he looked at Elizabeth. "What happened?"

"I got it working again."

"What?" he rose quickly and sat up. "Ow," he said putting a hand up to his head. "I have a cracking headache."

Elizabeth was prepared for that and gave him two paracetamol tablets.

"It was amazing. There are lots of memories I would have liked to have seen, what you were like as a kid looking in the mirror or being with you on your first date, lots of memories. She had a cheeky smile that faded. I was as quick as I could be and he's got his passphrase. We need to get out of here and quick."

At the top level Orlov was busy on the computer and Jani was on another.

"What about my mother?" she demanded.

"I lied," he said. "The drone could only stay up for twenty-four hours. Your mother is perfectly safe as I said she would be." He kept working away.

"We want to go outside for some fresh air, open the door Karl." said Daniel.

Orlov looked at the pair. "You're joking. You want to go outside? You'll not get very far without meeting some of Boris's friends I can assure you. And your friend Doctor Smith has left so there are only forests, tundra, lakes and volcanoes and of course bears," he shrugged. "Ok, I would suggest that you don't stray too far."

Orlov tapped his desk and a drawer opened. He pulled out two wristbands. "These are locators put them on. I will be able to find you if you get lost. You will not be able to remove them until I send an unlock code."

He clicked on his wristband activating Holovue and touched an icon. The door slowly slid open and the two went outside.

"Oh by the way Karl the laptop's in the lab. The password is p3pp3rp0t," said Elizabeth.

As the door was closing she could see Jani leaving her computer and heading for the elevator.

"What now?"

Daniel pointed upwards. "We have to get to the top of that volcano. Ian has flown off with the seaplane and left the Kolb."

He set off into the forest.

"Wait, are you crazy. I must have used up a lot of your neurons. Dan!"

"It's our only way out."

"You're nuts," she shouted.

They made their way through the forest whooping and calling to let the bears know to move off. Dense vegetation made progress slow but eventually they came out into a clearing leading to the slopes of the volcano and thankfully the forest was thinning out. A muffled bang echoed in the still air. They looked at each other.

"That could have been us if you hadn't been so switched on," said Daniel.

They turned and carried on up the slope. Elizabeth heard a distinctive noise that she had heard once before.

Orlov returned to his computer, his face was cold with rage. "Leaving a little parting gift Elizabeth, naughty, naughty," he said.

He drew up a 3D map of the surrounding countryside, punched in the locators causing a green dot to flash.

"Your luck's in Elizabeth. I still need you but not precious Daniel," he said launching a drone.

The armed drone appeared above the tree line. Its camera drew a box round Daniel face and a green light gave the go ahead. It began firing hitting Daniel on the shoulder. Elizabeth pulled him back down the slope into denser bushes but it still kept firing. The bullets were whining near and getting closer. Four Russian military helicopters flew directly overhead straight for Orlov's complex. The firing stopped and the drone flew off. Elizabeth and Daniel stood up to see the helicopters arriving above Orlov's complex and armed combat soldiers were abseiling down ropes to get to the ground. A fierce fire-fight between the increasing number of drones and the soldiers intensified.

"Come on let's keep going," said Daniel.

They could hear bears crashing through the forest below in fear running away from the fighting. As they increased height, vegetation gave way to rock and shingle. They were now in the open scrambling as fast as they could go. Daniel could feel the blood dripping down his chest as they finally neared the volcano's caldera rim. Exhausted they stopped for a moment and looked back. There was less firing now. A seaplane from a hidden boat house on the lake took off and within seconds a massive explosion engulfed the whole area knocking the helicopters out of the sky and killing anyone that might still have been alive. The ground shook several times. Elizabeth and Daniel reached the rim and looked down into the caldera. The Kolb sat on a patch of snow, but the snow was melting fast and many more sulphur and steam fumaroles were spraying upwards. The ground shook again. They staggered down from the rim to the Kolb. The loss of blood was having an effect on Daniel and he was having difficulty staying conscious. The sulphurous air was pungent catching the back of the throat.

"There are no doors," said Elizabeth alarmed.

Daniel slipped on the snow and collapsed groaning. Elizabeth picked him up and put him into the aircraft. She put on his harness and helmet and climbed in the other side doing the same. Ian had left a note.

"If you manage to get here, these are the instructions for flying the Kolb."

"Daniel," said Elizabeth. "Come on we have to go."

"I can't move my right arm and I'm feeling really dizzy. Elizabeth, you'll have to fly."

"What! Are you crazy?"

"You fly or we die."

There was a massive jolt causing the wings to dip almost touching the snow.

"Turn the key and keep it pressed until the engine starts. There, there." The engine burst into life.

"Get it up to 6000 revs."

Now there were fissures opening all over the place with steam and sulphur jets everywhere.

"Let the brake off. Here, here."

The Kolb shot forward sliding over the rapidly disappearing snow. Elizabeth screamed and looked back to see cracks opening in the ground.

"Look where you're going, slowly pull the stick back."

The plane lifted sharply and Elizabeth over compensated causing the aircraft to hit the ground with a crack.

"Ow slowly!" he said grimacing with pain.

This time the aircraft lifted gently, clear of the snow. By now the rim of the caldera was obscured by the fumaroles and steam that were joining up. They broke clear of the smoke to see the rim coming straight at them. Daniel and

Elizabeth screamed. She pulled the stick back and left and they just cleared the edge of the rim suddenly finding themselves thousands of feet up.

"Take it back to 4000 revs." Daniel looked at Elizabeth and thought. "That's my girl."

Behind them a large plume of smoke was coming from the volcano with small eruptions and ash spilling over the rim. Then there was a massive thunderous roar. Flames smoke and ash rose high up into the atmosphere with lava pouring down the sides of the volcano. A shock wave hit the small aircraft pushing it further away from the volcano. Fortunately they were flying into a head wind that was blowing all the ash and smoke the other way. Elizabeth took the aircraft lower to a less scary height of about 500 feet.

"There's a small cabin by a lake it's not far, about ten miles north-west." He shouted and then passed out. Elizabeth was beginning to understand the aircraft better and she was getting used to the responses to her handling of the controls.

"This wasn't so difficult after all," she thought.

Ruby woke early. Pale orangey light filtered through the net curtains of the log cabin. She had a feeling of well-being of self-satisfaction, happiness and contentment. She turned over and could it be true, you bet. There was special agent Brian Ross, asleep. Ruby wondered what the difference was between an agent and a special agent. Maybe the distinction was only in the cinema. He wasn't that much younger than her maybe seven years, so what. He was quite a private person and didn't talk about himself much. Was he married, who cares. Ruby smiled. What would her prudish daughter think about that? Was she in love with him, maybe. She got out of bed careful not to wake him opened the door and went out to the porch. The light was amazing painting a myriad of colours on the wonderful wild landscape.

"Thank you God," she said quietly. "Life's not so bad."

Elizabeth spotted a lake with a small cabin and aimed for it. Glancing to her left Daniel was still out of it. There had been so much fear and now it had all been used up, the fear factor had gone. With a renewed confidence in her ability to control the Kolb she started to descend towards the lake. Approaching the surface of the water the Kolb still seemed to be going too fast even with the stall warning speaker bleating. The Kolb hit the water and bounced, then again and again until the friction of the water against the rubber apron slowed the aircraft down. Without waiting for it to stop Elizabeth shut everything down took her helmet off and leaned back closing her eyes. The adrenalin had worn off leaving her exhausted. A gentle bumping motion woke Elizabeth opening her eyes. A clear night sky with a full moon lit the landscape with an eerie white light. The wind had gently pushed the aircraft onto a pumice beach below the cabin. It was very cold. Elizabeth shook Daniel.

"Dan." He groaned. "Come on let's get you up to the cabin."

Unfastening her seatbelt she looked behind her seat and next to her helmet was a rope. She stepped out of the aircraft onto a raft of pumice thinking it was the beach. The water was only a few inches deep but the shock of the unexpected cold water took her breath away. It was only a few steps to reach dry land. There was a ring on the bow of the rubber apron that Elizabeth tied the rope to. Pulling on the rope the light breeze coming from the lake helped her to drag the Kolb onto the beach and tighten it round the stake. Going round to Daniel's side of the aircraft she put her hand on his shoulder.

"Let's go Dan. Come on buddy you're going to have to help me out here, you're too heavy for me to carry."

With the harness unlatched and his helmet removed it was just a question of lifting one leg out then the other until Daniel was standing upright. With one arm over her shoulder and a firm hold of his waist, they both staggered up the beach towards the cabin. The door swung open. If Elizabeth was thinking of some kind of idealized cabin with a big hearth a large double bed and curtains she would have been sadly mistaken. The small outer room was used for storing wood with bags of vegetables hanging from hooks in the ceiling. A large metal sink stood against a wall under an old manual water pump. The inner door opened.

"What a dump," she said out loud.

To her left were two bunk beds adjacent to another two with just enough room to walk between them. She gently lowered Daniel onto a bottom bunk with a bare old mattress. Several voles squeaked and scurried from under the bed out of the door. To the right was a wood stove with two seats next to a small window. Conveniently, matches and some kindling were by the stove and in no time the cabin was heating up. Annoying biting mosquitoes appeared. Daniel was sleeping. Sitting on the opposite bunk and touching his uncharacteristically stubbly face there was no doubt in Elizabeth's mind that the female of the species has a difficult tightrope to walk whether it's a moth, bird of paradise, or a human. Ninety-nine per cent of their time is spent attracting the wrong kind of male and when the right male comes along, how do they know? Elizabeth knew. With difficulty she took off his jacket and shirt and with a strip from a pillow case dipped in water from the pump started to clean his wound. Lifting him gently there was no sign of an exit wound indicating that the bullet was still in the shoulder. He needed medical help. A search of the cabin didn't take long. There was plenty of wood and the bags hanging from the roof contained carrots onions and other vegetables. There were packets of dried soup and various dried meals and then hallelujah an old first aid kit had been left behind by the last occupant containing insect repellent. It had hardly been used.

"Whoever you are, thank you," she said spraying herself and Daniel.

Antiseptic sprays, bandages, painkillers, it was a treasure trove. "It's so beautiful here; I wonder what it's like in the winter," she thought. "Come on," she said to herself, "I'd better hide the Kolb. There will be a lot of people anxiously looking for us for one reason or another."

It was surprisingly easy to manoeuvre it next to some Dwarf Pine and then cutting the bushes until she covered the plane until it was hidden. A weird soup, stew mixture was bubbling away on the stove. Cooking had never been her thing but it did smell good and through the dirty window a new dawn was beginning. Opening the door of the stove with an oven glove and putting another log in closing the door, she sighed. The eastern sky was beginning to lighten.

"Life's not so bad."

The screen on the wall of the Chief of the SIS was showing a news channel's pictures of a volcanic eruption in Kamchatka. Hollinger drummed the table with his fingers while his left hand held a secure phone to his ear.

"Prime Minister we're monitoring Eastern Russia's Television Network and they're showing aerial images of a Volcanic explosion very close to Orlov's compound. Our analysts are still studying them but preliminary reports suggest that where Orlov's location co-ordinates were there is nothing left. It looks like there has been a massive explosion at the site. It's possible it could have been responsible for triggering the nearby volcanic eruption."

He turned to look out of the window at the floating restaurants meandering down the Thames River.

"The Russians are furious because they have lost an entire crack combat team including four Mil Mi-24 gunship attack helicopters and privately they're blaming us. That's thirty-two troops and eight pilots. Of course they can't blame us publicly otherwise that would be an admission that they were intercepting our communications. They've summoned our Ambassador to the Kremlin and he received a right royal dressing down. They have also withdrawn his Excellency the Russian ambassador here, probably temporarily. I'm afraid we have no definitive information but the short answer is no, there are no survivors. Even if there were from the initial explosion, nobody in that area could have survived the volcanic blast. It was massive. So that leaves us with the intriguing prospect that our problems are at an end. It is highly likely that Orlov, Graham and Stanford are all dead. We would never be able to verify it because there is literally nothing left but a big hole in the ground. Yes Sir."

Hollinger put the phone down and watched the newsreel.

7

"I'm not a great believer that scientists should agonize over the morality of their work."

A black sedan picked its way along a winding road through the strange ghost forests in the Yosemite National Park. The Lodge Pole Pine trees had been stripped of their bark and bleached white by an invasion of small Needleminer moths. It continued its journey emerging from the bleak colourless landscape into the lush green giant Sequoia forest until eventually arriving at a wooden cabin. Ruby and Brian were waiting at the porch.

"Gentlemen would you like some coffee?" asked Ruby.

"No thanks Ma'am we can't stay. Agent Ross," he acknowledged Brian's presence. "Ma'am I'm afraid we have some bad news about your daughter."

Ruby touched Brian's arm and put a hand to her mouth.

"We have strong evidence to suggest that Doctor Graham was killed in an explosion."

"How can that be possible? When? Where? I don't understand," she said.

"I'm sorry Ms Graham for national security reasons all I can tell you is that it happened yesterday."

"What about her body?"

He shook his head. "We don't have that."

"Well then how can you be so sure?"

"I'm sorry I can't tell you that either. There is no longer any need to stay here now Ma'am. Agent Ross you'll escort Ms Graham back home," and with that they got back into the car and drove away.

"I'm so sorry Ruby."

He held onto her as the tears flowed.

The early morning sun was rising, suspended over the glacial lake creating a perfect mirror reflection. Daniel was sitting on a bench outside the cabin. He was feeling a lot better after his night's sleep. Elizabeth came out with two elaborately decorated plates of the stew she had made earlier and sat down next to him.

"Hey this looks good, interesting plates."

They had a myriad of tiny rose petals connected with lines of gilding getting smaller and smaller in concentric circles disappearing under the stew.

"Remember Monique, head chef from La Belle Époque?" he asked.

"Nope, haven't been there."

"Ah must've been Rhona. She wouldn't serve you with anything other than a white plate. Bit of a foodie snob, excellent food though. She took an artistic pride in it I asked her why it was always a white plate once. '*Anyzing else eez like painting ze Mona Lisa on ze tartan table cloth.*' I didn't know you could cook like that, delicious."

Daniel licked his spoon. He was obviously getting better.

"I'm not particularly good at cooking, just got lucky I guess. I've been having a scout around. There's a single wire electric fence all the way along the perimeter but it doesn't include the latrine," said Elizabeth.

"I know," he said.

Elizabeth had found some coffee and they sat quietly enjoying each other's company. Daniel began to relate the events of the past few days. How he had found the clue about Orlov. He told her all about Adak Island and landing the seaplane in the volcano, until Elizabeth was up to date.

"We have a lot of thinking to do." Daniel stood up.

"Hey take it easy you've still got a bullet in you."

"I'm feeling a lot better and I've got the use of my arm back."

He leaned against the cabin wall and looked over the lake. Elizabeth studied the coffee in her cup.

She stood up. "Do you remember hearing the bomb in my laptop explode, that must have been Jani. I saw her leave Orlov when we were at the door. And I saw what must have been Orlov escape in a seaplane seconds before the compound explosion. You were somewhat distracted by the bullet in your shoulder at the time. There are two positive things that we can take out of our situation now," she said. "One we're still alive and two, everybody thinks we're dead."

"When that huge bomb went off it must have killed all those soldiers. The Kremlin will be seriously displeased at our friend Orlov," said Daniel.

"I hid the Kolb," said Elizabeth.

"Thank goodness for that they'll be looking for him everywhere. They'll never accept that he died in the blast he's not the suicide type. We can't stay here, someone will check out the cabin eventually and we can't fly to Petropavlovsk it's too far. There's a marine research station further north. Ian was working on salmon research there a while ago and I did some research for my PhD. It's right on the coast. I may have one or two friends still there that could help us."

Elizabeth put her cup down. "What are we going to do when we get to the research station? Where will we go?"

Daniel took her hand. "I don't know. For once I've run out of ideas. When we get there, maybe by then something will come to me. Perhaps we should take on new identities and go and live in California or Costa Rica or Cape Town. I know how to grow grapes and make wine. What do you think?"

"Don't be ridiculous." Elizabeth got up and went into the outer room. "I'm not giving up my job and my life in London. We have to have a plan to sort all this mess out, to get back our lives. I dragged you into this I'm sorry."

"What are you doing?"

"I'm looking for something."

What?"

"This."

Elizabeth came back in holding a pair of very old rusting bolt cutters and easily removed the locators.

"Perversely, I think if it hadn't been for Orlov I doubt whether you and me would be alive today. The British government had no qualms about ending your life and mine. Elizabeth, Orlov's copy of your work is presumably gone and I doubt whether he will be able to hack the CIA again that means the CIA and GCHQ have the same files and folders but without you they don't make any sense. SIS may have your hard drive but that's encrypted and again only you know how it works. The only danger you pose to them is if the International intelligence community know about you and one of them force you to spend as long as it takes to recreate your work. So logically if we could somehow open a channel of communication with Hollinger, we could persuade him to protect you and the project."

"Can we trust him? Wait we've forgotten that Orlov has the SIS master passphrase," said Elizabeth.

"We'll have to speak to Hollinger and quick," he said.

"You saved our lives Elizabeth, getting us out of the volcano. You're very brave" He looked at her and smiled. "Hey I thought you couldn't fly."

"Just got lucky I guess."

Hollinger looked down at the Thames traffic. He was always fascinated by the variety of river borne craft the flotsam and jetsam of life coming and going night and day and it helped him think.

Something was nagging him. He knew the feeling well. Gut feeling, intuition, hunch, instinct, whatever you want to call it but it was there and it wasn't going away. He had learned in the end to respect this feeling but it didn't change the endless battle between logic and intuition. He was good at his job. There were many in the intelligence community wary of him and his power but most of all his intellect and depth of perception. He wasn't convinced that the answer was always a simple political one, to be solved and move on to the next one. It was all about people. He would have made a brilliant CEO of any company. Not because of projections, not because of stats and spread sheets. There were plenty of people who would understand these things better. No, it was because he understood people. He understood how to motivate, inspire. He understood aspirations, failings, desires, and weaknesses, how to exploit, how to negate. His hero was Sir Alex Ferguson though he had no interest in football but that wasn't the point, Sir Alex knew a thing or two about the human psyche.

During a few rudimentary lessons Ian had told Daniel *'if you can drive a car you can fly a Kolb'* and so it proved. The Kolb flew north hugging the coast line beneath a towering cliff face a dozen or so yards above the surf. Giant otters stopped crunching shellfish held on their bellies while floating on the water, to watch the plane fly over. Seabirds nesting on the cliffs took fright filling the sky as the aircraft flew by. Guillemots and razorbills bounced off the screen protecting the rotor until Daniel tracked out to sea a little to avoid the nesting birds. Horned and Tufted Puffins, Crested, Parakeets and Whiskered Auklets wheeled around the aircraft in distress and eventually were left behind. Daniel started to climb. A waterfall cascading from a lake adjacent to the cliffs fell hundreds of feet into the sea. On the edge of the lake the research station was a small settlement of basic cabins and Portakabins. He touched down on the surface of the lake and taxied to a pier. The aircraft was securely tied to a wooden stanchion and they walked along the boards towards the station. There was no sign of anyone except for music coming from the small communal hall. As they entered unnoticed a large group of researchers and their families were celebrating the end of the season's work. Soon it would be homeward bound before winter set in. Two dogs were fighting and in the process of pulling them apart the lights fused and the music coming from a ghetto blaster stopped. In the gloom of the hall tables were lined with small bottles of vodka mostly empty and half eaten plates of food. The silence was broken by a cry.

"Daniel!"

A large blonde woman threw her arms around him and kissed him full on the lips.

"Ow," he said holding his shoulder.

"Where have you been you bad boy?" she said thinking he was joking.

Elizabeth tapped her on the arm and said, "with me."

Ignoring her she clung on to Daniel. "Where's Ian?"

"That's a long story Anna. This is Elizabeth. We need your help, can we talk somewhere quiet."

The three of them entered Anna's cabin. A stove kept the room warm. Daniel was still holding his shoulder.

"Sit down," she said. "Are you hurt?"

"I took a bullet in my shoulder it's still there."

Anna took out her phone and spoke in Russian then put it back into her pocket. "It sounds serious how can I help?"

Daniel took off his jacket and sat down.

"For your own sake, the least you know the better. I need to communicate with London."

"Normally that would be easy. We had a very fast satellite linked broadband connection here but all of our equipment has been dismantled and shipped out. So you will have to go to Petropavlovsk."

Someone knocked and a head popped round the door.

"Elena come in, this is a good friend of mine Daniel and his friend Ellis."

"Ellis?" said Elizabeth.

"Daniel has a bullet in his shoulder. Elena is an excellent veterinarian. She hasn't lost a patient yet. A seaplane will arrive tomorrow, you can travel in that. Now I must get back to my friends. If there's anything else just ask," she said closing the door.

Daniel took off his blood stained shirt. Elena opened a bag and took out a rolled up cloth that she unrolled to reveal various surgical tools. She cleaned the wound with a mild antibacterial wash and took out a hypodermic with a small phial of anaesthetic. She plunged the needle into the phial and withdrew it making sure there were no bubbles and injected Daniel in the shoulder.

"This is local," she said. "I understand English, no speak well."

She made Daniel lie on the couch and waited while the anaesthetic worked. Then she took the forceps and starting probing into Daniels wound soon finding what she was looking for and pulled out the bullet.

"Souvenir," she said smiling and handed it to Daniel.

The wound was cleaned again and expertly dressed with a pad and surgical tape. Elena took off her pullover and her shirt much to Elizabeth's surprise, revealing her bra. She handed the shirt to Daniel.

"Take," she said. "You need." And put on her pullover.

"Bolshoe spasibo," said Daniel.

Elena blushed as she packed up her medicine bag. "I must go. Sauna is ready, last one before leave."

"Sauna?" asked Elizabeth.

"You like?" said Elena. "Is women children."

"Yes."

"Come," then pointing at Daniel, "you stay."

In the sixties it was a Soviet Navy twin-engine maritime reconnaissance, anti-submarine warfare flying-boat. Now the converted Beriev Be-12 was overloaded but that didn't seem to bother the pilot who stayed in the cockpit looking at maps and checking the instruments and the weather. There was only room for Daniel, Elizabeth and a third of the research staff with their families. Every available space was taken up. Even the aisle was packed with equipment and luggage. Live chickens clucked in wicker baskets and a couple of piglets held by twin girls squealed. The line attached to the pier was cast off and the pilot started the engines. It seemed dangerously low in the water. The pilot went to full throttle and it leapt forward. Feathers from the basket floated around the cabin and after what seemed like forever it took off. When they arrived at Petropavlovsk Airport, Anna led them into a small office with a computer and Daniel sat down. He found an email address for SIS on the web and started typing.

Hollinger's computer signalled that an email had arrived via admin. He clicked on it and the message appeared.

'FAO Sir Anthony Hollinger
Sir Anthony this may come as a surprise to you
but Elizabeth and I are very much alive. So is
Orlov and he possesses the SIS master passphrase
so be warned.'

Hollinger immediately picked up the phone. "George, call Dame Amelia and tell her the master passphrase has been breached and inform the various departments right away."

'The explosives in the laptop intended for Elizabeth
detonated killing a woman who worked for Orlov.
We want to do a deal. We will come to London but
you must guarantee our safety. Elizabeth wishes to
place the Remembrance Project and herself under
the protection of the UK Government with certain
conditions. We are at Petropavlovsk Airport.
Daniel Stanford.'

Hollinger forwarded it to Dame Amelia Sharp and called the Cabinet Secretary.

Daniel thanked Anna and they said their goodbyes. There was a small cafeteria where they ordered Russian Blinchiki. The pancakes came with strong Russian Caravan black tea.

"Remember the London taxi driver and your funny money?" he asked.

"Yes, he was rude about it and I was annoyed he said something about Monopoly money."

"Our meeting was arranged by grand design you know, fate, destiny. We had fun then, didn't we?" asked Daniel.

"We were young then," said Elizabeth.

"It wasn't that long ago."

"Young in mind."

"I'm still young in mind."

Elizabeth laughed. "Yes you certainly are, don't change."

They watched a private jet land and taxi to the terminal.

"I wonder how long we're going to be here," she said.

A flight attendant lowered the stairs and stepped down. The door of the café opened and he looked around then came over.

"Mr and Mrs Smith?" he asked. They looked at each other. "That would be Mr Daniel and Mrs Elizabeth Smith."

"Yes," they said in unison.

"Good. Your aircraft is being refuelled so in about twenty minutes we will be ready to go."

Having finished the Blinchiki they paid in dollars and walked out to the jet. It was an RAF HS125 CC3 VIP jet aircraft. As they climbed the steps they saw a small private jet take off with darkened windows.

"You guys are really lucky." A uniformed man was at the top of the stairs. "We were on route to Brize Norton when we were diverted to pick you up. This aircraft is normally used for the royal family. Welcome onboard."

The interior was understated and classy. "My father would have liked this," said Elizabeth.

It was quite small with mushroom coloured leather seats. Elizabeth and Daniel sat down as the steward closed the door. Almost immediately the engines fired up and they were taxiing onto the runway.

"When we reach cruising height, there will be drinks available hot and cold and a choice of menu."

"What a strange life you lead," said Daniel.

Orlov and Jani touched down on the tarmac at the Milkovo airstrip. She had survived the blast by using a small example of the latest airline Fly-bag designed to contain explosions on an aircraft. He taxied onto the grass next to a hanger. Within seconds he had secured a connection on his smart phone and clicked a few icons. At Petropavlovsk airport, a small black pilotless jet's engines started up. The on board computer filed a flight plan to Milkovo and because there was little traffic received immediate clearance to take off. Within two minutes it was airborne and in fifteen minutes it was landing again. Orlov and Jani waited for it to stop and walked briskly out. Face recognition scanners checked out the pair as they approached then the door opened and the steps came down. They sat on white leather seats helped themselves to drinks, fastened seat belts as Orlov filed a new flight plan. The jet took off and reached 33,000 feet before levelling off. Orlov finished his drink and switched on the satellite news channel while Jani prepared a hot dish in the galley.

Breaking news was all about the Kizimen Volcano explosion with helicopter film of huge plumes of smoke and ash thousands of feet in the atmosphere above. Molten rock was rolling down its sides. Orlov had always known that at some point his base in Kamchatka would end and that's why he had chosen with great care to have a backup base. The attraction for remote areas persisted. They were heading for Dornabay a remote island off the west coast of Scotland. With no people and no houses, it was ideal. The attraction apart from its remoteness was that beneath the ground it had a series of connected cold war nuclear fall-out shelters abandoned, long forgotten and a very long hard sandy beach. Orlov had completely revamped the space in a near copy of the compound at Kamchatka. It would take thirteen hours to reach Scotland. Orlov switched on the computer and the news channel disappeared.

He immediately hacked into GCHQ servers using the master passphrase and began downloading and transferring gigabytes of data when the screen turned red with the words.

'UNAUTHORIZED CONNECTION TERMINATED.'

"That's strange," he thought.

Ruby was paying for a bag of doughnuts at her local grocery store as two men entered and approached her. They waited until she had received change from a $10 bill and one tapped her lightly on the shoulder. She turned in surprise to see agent Brian Ross and agent Stenner both wearing a smile. Brian took her elbow gently and whispered.

"Got some good news Ruby, let's go out to the car."

He opened the back door letting her in and closed the door while Stenner sat in front with the driver. Brian climbed in and closed the door giving her a kiss on the cheek. They joined the traffic and headed south.

"Elizabeth's Ok."

"What?"

"We were wrong. Based on the information we had at the time, it was the only conclusion we could make but Daniel and Elizabeth are safe."

Ruby started crying and threw her arms round Brian to his embarrassment. The driver glanced in the mirror.

"But it means we're going to have to take you right now to a safe house again."

Ruby took out a handkerchief and dried her tears.

"Well it wasn't so bad the last time." She said.

Orlov knew the tide would be out not that it mattered because the jet had vertical landing capability. Flying over the island there was nothing to see but natural vegetation. Impossible to see was a well camouflaged satellite dish. Orlov had switched off the transponder earlier and changed course making the jet invisible to air traffic controllers. The graphene fuselage had no radar signature. The pilotless computer controlled jet flew round the island reducing speed and headed for the glistening sandy beach. Spectacular sprays of seawater followed the aircraft as it touched down. It taxied towards a rising slip below what looked like a large domed boat shed covered with a turfed roof. It had taken several years using foreign labour to achieve his goal of a command and control centre hidden underground. Orlov didn't waste any time powering up the control room with its banks of monitors served by the latest quantum computer he had engineered and built himself. He searched the hard drive and brought up the hacked files, quickly finding Hollinger's email account. The very last email that Hollinger had just received was from...Daniel Stanford. Orlov shot forward to read the email. He put his head in his hands and screamed. With supreme effort he cooled the red mist and kept it simmering under control. He scanned Hollinger's emails searching for his name and up came a message sent to the British Ambassador to Russia in Moscow.

"So that's how they knew," he said grimly. "Well Sir Anthony Hollinger, you want to play games? Let the games commence."

They taxied towards a VIP section of RAF Brize Norton's passenger terminal. As the engine noise subsided the door opened and the stairs glided into place. Daniel and Elizabeth the only two passengers were met on the tarmac by a waiting car that took them to a helicopter with the rotors turning. Within seconds of clicking on their seatbelts, it took off for the highly secret and heavily defended United Kingdom Government Military Science Park at Porton Down. Set in 7,000 acres of land near Salisbury, its home to the Defence Science and Technology Laboratory. (Dstl) Research includes chemical, biological, radiological and nuclear (CBRN) defence. Daniel and Elizabeth were ushered into meeting room three. A group of men and women standing at the far end of the room turned round. A tall thin man with grey hair and spectacles perched on his nose came forward.

"Doctor Graham and Professor Stanford," he said. "I finally get to meet you, Anthony Hollinger I'm glad you got here safely. Please have a seat."

He beckoned towards the nearest of eight round a table. The others took their seats on cue.

"You tried to kill me with a bomb in my laptop," said Elizabeth grimly. There was an embarrassing silence.

"Yes. I apologise. The circumstances at the time dictated drastic measures. Let me start the introductions. I'm Director General of SIS."

"John Mitchell, Head of Operations, Centre for Defence Enterprise."

"Sir Joseph Babcock, Chairman of Defence Science and Technology Laboratory."

"Allan Smyth, Technical and Strategy Director, Dstl."

"Colin Stone, Chief Executive, Dstl."

"Penny Anderson, People and Business Services Director, Dstl."

"Dame Amelia Sharp, Head of GCHQ." Sharp started off the meeting. "Can I thank you Daniel, may I call you Daniel?" Dan nodded, "for letting us know about the breech in GCHQ servers. They are now secure thanks to you, but," she hesitated. "How did Orlov get the master passphrase?"

Elizabeth touched Daniels hand. "I don't know how much we should be saying here," she said.

Hollinger rubbed his chin. "Everyone here has an up to date Developed Vetting clearance. That's the highest security clearance."

Elizabeth pulled a strand of red hair from her face. "As incredible as it may seem, I had successfully accessed human memory." There was a gasp from those who had not known. "There were five copies of the computer programme. Number one is still illegally held by the CIA. Number two is illegally held by GCHQ. Number three was blown up at my lab at the NRC in London. Number four was my laptop and number five was Orlov's stolen copy from the CIA that I was forced to work on in Kamchatka. I used it to trace Daniel's memories of the time when he had once worked with SIS. He knew that Daniel would have had access to the master passphrase. So he used me to see through Daniels eyes." The room was silent. "It is not unlike playing a tape. It may also be possible to wipe the memory."

"Quite extraordinary," said Babcock. "This would be cataclysmic in the wrong hands."

"Quite. But your wrong Elizabeth, we have the hard drive from your laptop," said Hollinger.

"The thing is I didn't expect for a moment that when I started working on the Remembrance programme that it could be used for military purposes, something I am absolutely against. It is far too dangerous. It could threaten every single person living on the planet."

Hollinger knew the answer to his question. It was for the others to hear the answer.

"What do you propose?"

"I want the stolen programmes destroyed. I need a cast iron guarantee that Remembrance will not be used by the military. If you give me back my laptop hard drive I will rebuild the programme. The user interface will be simplified and once it's all together." Elizabeth held Daniels hand. "Daniel will remove all the project construction memories from my brain so that I will not be able to build another. It's my view that Remembrance could be a tool to help millions of people. I may be able to build in safeguards to stop its military capability but if not I accept that it may have to be destroyed."

Babcock looked at Mitchell and back at Elizabeth.

"We are all here for a free and frank discussion. Elizabeth has created something that's hard to believe. It's like science fiction. But I'm not a great believer that scientists should agonize over the morality of their work. On July 16, 1945 the first atomic bomb was detonated in New Mexico after which J. Robert Oppenheimer said;"

'Now I am become Death, the destroyer of worlds.'

"Don't tell me he didn't know what he was doing and what the results might be because he did. Now if we could turn the clock back and Oppenheimer came in here and said hey guys I've developed a weapon so powerful that a single bomb can destroy a whole city but it's far too dangerous to ever be used let's destroy all the research. Would the world be any safer? No, why? Because some other clever scientist would have taken his place by now only it could be a regime hostile to the west. I'm not meaning to cause offence but what I'm saying is that Elizabeth is a very clever and talented scientist and she created something that may never be repeatable in our lifetime. The question for everyone around this table is can we take that gamble?"

This wasn't the reaction Elizabeth expected and she looked at Hollinger with alarm as the grip on Daniels hand became firmer. A strange awkward silence hung in the room like a bad smell. Hollinger got up to break the tension and opened a window.

Elizabeth looked at Hollinger. "I didn't expect this, did you know?"

"Know? No but I would have been very surprised if it hadn't been brought up."

Elizabeth wasn't having this. "Sir Alastair, The question you ask is rather nebulous since there is no we but if I was to answer it anyway my answer is yes I am prepared to take the gamble. Sir Anthony, I thought we had an understanding. Do we still have that?"

"Well we had sorry have an understanding and if I'm speaking personally, it would be yes but of course I would have to consult the Prime Minister."

Daniel stood up. "I don't think you're quite getting the message. If we don't have a cast iron agreement here and now, there will be no work done on this project."

"Well then Joseph," said Hollinger. "I think you've got your answer. We'll just have to take that gamble." Daniel sat down.

Hollinger put his hands together "Now let's get down to business. Penny Anderson will look after all your needs, show you the living quarters where to eat, get clothes for you. Because you will not be leaving Porton Down until it's all over. Allan Smyth will supply any technical expertise, equipment, whatever you need. Are there any questions?" he looked round the room. "Good!"

They all filed out leaving Hollinger and a very tired Daniel and Elizabeth who were still sitting down.

"Your mother knows you are Ok and she's safe. The CIA is looking after her."

He patted Elizabeth on the shoulder and left.

8

"I'm afraid I'm going to have to concentrate your mind a little on the expediency of the matter in hand."

It was two in the morning and the telephone rang waking up Hollinger. The bedside lamp wouldn't switch on. He fumbled around and found the phone.

"Yes, yes, Ok."

He pressed the end call button and dialled for his driver. The route to 70 Whitehall was completely dark. "This is what it must have been like during the blitz." He thought. The COBRA meeting was already in progress when he arrived and the deputy Chief of SIS was beginning to brief the meeting.

"The situation is extremely serious. Sixteen operational nuclear reactors at all nine plants in the country have had to be shut down because their computers have been breached. That's a loss of almost twenty per cent of electricity produced. None of the reactors are damaged but it will take days to get them back on line. That's the good news. Whoever did this and I think we can be pretty certain it's Orlov could have caused the equipment to do just about anything he wanted. Apart from the complete destruction of the nuclear power plants, he could have caused environmental damage laying waste to large parts of the country. This is just a shot across the bows, an Orlov warning."

Hollinger spoke for the first time. "Prime Minister if this is a warning then there is something he wants and he's softening us up for the demand."

PM scratched his head. "What is it he wants and do we have any idea where he is?"

Hollinger replied. "We have no idea where he is. As to what he wants, I think we'll find out soon enough. It may be a certain Doctor Elizabeth Graham."

Orlov always had a soft spot for Scotland principally through his long association with single malt whisky. Any country that could create so wonderful a drink must be alright. He and Jani were sitting at a large desk of polished Caithness stone on metal supports watching SBC TV's satellite news channel on a single large 8k touch screen, the news presenter was speculating on the causes of the power cuts. It was clear that the government was keeping quiet for now.

"Let's get out of here Jani." She got up and put her arm around him.

"What did you have in mind?"

Orlov hit a master switch and everything shut down.

"Just a little diversion," he said.

They stepped into the elevator and after a short ascent it opened. A narrow corridor led to the small camouflaged hanger containing the jet and a jet-boat on a trailer. He pressed a large green button and the doors opened. The trailer was lowered down the slipway until it reached the water. Orlov picked up a backpack while Jani untied the boat, walked down the slipway and jumped on to the craft. She pushed off and jumped on. He pressed an icon on the Holovue wristband and the door closed. Taking out her binoculars Jani scanned along the coast. Scores of armed drone-skimmers rested on shallow rock pools and beaches around the island to conserve power. Orlov developed the technology by observing pond skimmers walking on water. He engineered the curved legs of the drones rotating inward and downward with just enough force to take off pushing against the surface tension without breaking through. They were part of Orlov's tactical defend and secure assets. Measuring four feet across and eighteen inches high and made from his favourite material graphene. They were mounted with oval dome shaped recoilless firing mechanisms containing 12 laser guided. .380 calibre bullets. Once in attack mode they were completely autonomous and could adopt swarm behaviour. Aware of their surroundings they use motion sensors and thermal imaging to home in on the target within fifteen hundred feet. They could move fast at up to 30 miles an hour. Using his Holovue he put the skimmers into passive mode as Jani fired up the onboard engines which murmured beneath them.

"Let's head west," he said.

The surface of the water had that oily calm slack tide look. She turned the boat round pointing it to the horizon and took off. It could do 60 knots in the right conditions. Within twenty minutes Scotland had slipped below the horizon. Orlov took over and slowed down switched the engine off and let her drift. Jani opened a cooler and took a couple of beers opening them. He took the bottle and calculated there was probably another two hours of daylight.

"Do you miss Africa Jani? I do."

He finished assembling the fishing rod and was soon casting the line into the water.

"Yes," she said.

There was hardly any wind, perfect conditions for fishing.

"What do you miss most?"

Orlov was sitting on a seat at the stern with his feet on the edge of the boat.

"I miss everything. I miss my friends, the weather, the food and the doves in the acacia trees. I miss the wildness, the lions roaring at night. Do you remember the night we slept in the open round a fire under the Yellow Fever trees? There were baboons screaming above us being hunted by a leopard. I can hear them now."

"How could I forget? That was in the Ngorongoro crater and the next day four lionesses killed that huge buffalo. It took them a long time. They were so exhausted they couldn't eat for a while."

"Can we ever go back?"

"I hope so but for now I'm caught Jani. I can't change my destiny, maybe destiny will change me."

They sat there all alone in the stillness of an empty sea, relaxing to a soothing gentle movement of the boat. This was the first time for ages that he had found his inner calmness. Fishing was a form of meditation for him. He could keep all thoughts negative and otherwise at bay, an emptiness that refreshed the soul. There was a pull on the line.

"Quick, you've caught something," said Jani as the rod bent.

It had a hefty breaking strain of ten pounds. He pushed the end of the rod into a holder and let out some slack. He felt the line go slack again which he responded to by winding it in. The rod bent again, more violently this time and he released some more slack. This continued for an hour as the sun turning a blood red approached the horizon. He was getting tired and still the fish fought but he could tell it was tiring too. As the sun dipped below the horizon on the West a full moon was rising in the East.

"Here you have a go." Jani took over while Orlov took two more beers out.

She had been watching his technique and continued reeling the fish in. It was big and putting up a fight but it was no match for Jani. She reeled in the line. There was little resistance now as Orlov prepared the landing net. The fish surfaced for the first time and Orlov recognised that it was a huge Atlantic Bluefin tuna. He lifted the net and caught the tuna pulling it on board. It had a PSAT— pop-up satellite archival tag attached, probably by Dunstaffnage.

Orlov sighed. "He's tagged. He put up a good fight, shall we let him go? I think he deserves it."

Jani nodded. She unhooked the tuna and heaved it back into the water. He sat back in his chair, pulled a cigar out and for the first in an age lit it up took a puff and blew it out into the moonlit night sky. Jani enjoyed the smell of the cigar. She was pleased to see Orlov looking so relaxed.

The emergency generators seamlessly kicked in at Porton Down. Elizabeth and Daniel were cocooned and oblivious to what was happening on the outside. She thought that he should go back to his office at the NRC but Daniel argued that he wouldn't have been able to get in touch with her. So with very little to do he was spending a lot of time in the gym exercising while Elizabeth worked in the laboratory. Then Hollinger arrived. Security informed Daniel and he went straight to Elizabeth's laboratory.

"Elizabeth, Daniel. There have been a series of attacks on Britain by Orlov. He has shut down every single nuclear power station we have and he could do worse. We have just received a demand from him. He doesn't specify exactly what his next act would be but he's clear that if you are not handed over to him he will destroy Britain's infrastructure and it seems like he is perfectly capable of doing just that."

Elizabeth sat down. "If I was dead would that be an end to it?" The question shocked both listeners.

"Yes but objectively I really believe that's not the answer," said Hollinger.

"I want to see my mum," said Elizabeth.

"What?" asked Hollinger, "there is not a great deal of time."

"I want to see my mum," she repeated.

Hollinger sighed. He opened his tablet and pressed a link. Scanning down a list of names he found who he was looking for. Major General Sir Alexander Parris appeared on his monitor.

"Alex, I'm glad I manage to get hold of you, I need to ask a very, very big favour."

"Of course, who do you want blown up?" he smiled.

"No it's nothing like that," Hollinger wasn't blessed with a sense of humour. "I need to fly a civilian to a secure airfield near San Francisco and it has to be as quick as possible."

"You're not asking much are you? Let's see," he consulted a monitor out of view. "There's a LAPCAT A3 fuelled and on standby at Brize Norton, and the best place to land is Travis Air Force Base near San Francisco. Anthony no one has flown in the LAPCAT yet and there isn't much time for induction. Is she fit and well?"

"Yes, she is a remarkable woman," he looked over at Elizabeth. "How do you feel about flying hypersonic?"

"I don't know."

"Well, you're going to find out quite soon. Thanks Alex and if you can let our opposite numbers know, that would be marvellous?" he said ending the call.

"Oh by the way Elizabeth once you're airborne the flight time is about an hour and I should point out that the LAPCAT A3 is pilotless."

Brian was eating a raspberry ripple on the veranda of a hired houseboat moored in Sausalito near San Francisco and Ruby was pondering the next chess move when his mobile beeped.

"You're kidding me. Yeah, yeah Ok. Are you sure?" He looked at Ruby and smiled. "Ok" He put his mobile away. "Ruby I've got some good news."

"Check." She said.

"Ruby?"

"It's your move. What news?" she said.

Brian moved a bishop. "Elizabeth has arranged to see you."

"What, that's wonderful where?"

"She's flying to Travis Air Force Base. We've arranged for you to be picked up by helicopter from here, in fact it's on its way now and it will take you there."

"Are you not coming?"

"Sure," he said.

"Oh I'm so looking forward to seeing her, wonderful." She moved her queen, "checkmate."

Orlov was busy hacking into Comsbird 3 a geostationary communications satellite that combines with the ADS-b Global air control system processing and relaying communications between air traffic control systems and pilots. It turned out to be a soft target with poor defences and didn't take him long. He was a little disappointed at how easy it was. He reverse engineered access and changed passphrases so that no one but him could take control. Every air traffic controller relied heavily on the accuracy of this satellite and now his ownership was complete. With absolute control Orlov, could reposition the satellite or send it out of orbit crashing to the ground, impersonate an aircraft or send malicious and misleading information to control towers. Identify VIP jets like the Queens flight No. 32 (The Royal) Squadron and track its movement with details of logged flight plans. There was no end of mischief he could get up to. Comsbird 3 has a linked network connecting it to Comsbird 1, 2 and 4 and Orlov entered the open 'back door' dismantling their defences and substituting his encrypted keys. He now had control of them as well enabling him to wreak havoc around the world. He leaned back in his chair and put his feet up on the Caithness slate table. He owned four valuable satellites and it felt good but with ownership comes responsibility.

"I'll not be too tough just yet," he thought, "just another timely warning."

Orlov delved deeper into the satellite data base and instructions. He could see that Heathrow was experiencing a particularly busy period. He shut down all traffic from the Heathrow tower. Panic ensued. Immediately controllers and pilots were flying blind. Flights were immediately diverted and a string of cancellations appeared on the notice board as planes were grounded. Orlov counted the seconds then after exactly one minute he restored communications. Thirty seven near misses were logged by sweating air traffic controllers.

Travis Air Force Base was busy with military planes and helicopters taking off and landing regularly. The VIP room in a building near the tower was modestly furnished with arm chairs a couple of sofas and a large coffee table with magazines. Around the walls were lots of photographs of various military aircraft, some in flight some on the ground. Against the wall was a drinks trolley with three vacuum flasks and a plate of chocolate chip cookies covered with cling film. Below was a chill with various soft drinks and bottled water. Ruby and Brian were on their third coffee when the door burst open.

"Mum."

Elizabeth threw her arms round Ruby and they hugged each other as tears began to flow. Brian looked away slightly embarrassed or perhaps it was because he felt a little emotional as well. They sat on the sofa and Brian pored Elizabeth some coffee.

"This is CIA agent Ross," said Ruby. "Brian's been looking after me. He's a wonderful bodyguard. We were in Yosemite. It was fantastic being there. And then they told us that you were dead. My whole world crashed. I'm so glad to see you. We're being kept in the dark, I have absolutely no idea what's going on. Tell me are you Ok."

"Yes I'm fine mum."

"Can you tell me what happened?"

"Well, I was kidnapped in London and taken to Eastern Russia. Daniel thought he knew who could have done it and that gave him an idea where I might be and well a lot of things happened but we manage to get away and had to walk through a forest full of grizzly bears up a volcano where there was a small plane inside a caldera on some snow and then Russian troops arrived down below and there was a big gunfight and then there was a huge explosion that woke up the volcano, oh and Dan got shot in the shoulder, and I flew the plain out of the volcano as it erupted."

Ruby Looked at Elizabeth like a mother looks at a child that still believes in fairies.

"Yes dear. You've been working far too much," she said giving Elizabeth a big hug. "You need a break. You and Dan ought to go on a nice holiday somewhere. Come to the States we could go over to San Francisco, mm?"

Elizabeth smiled. "Yes mum, we will."

Hollinger and Sharp arrived at number 10 and were immediately ushered into the cabinet room to be met by the Cabinet Secretary, Angus MacDonald.

"The PM will be with you shortly and may I say that this is a very delicate situation requiring a great deal of care and pragmatism. Already a number of people have unnecessarily died. I know the PM is undecided but sometimes a sacrifice must be made for the greater good don't you think. Would you like a sherry or perhaps something a little stronger?"

"No thank you Angus and may I say that the only person between us and Armageddon is Doctor Elizabeth Graham. Now be a good boy and don't be filling the PM's head with disingenuous nonsense. If this goes wrong we're all done for."

"Sir Anthony thanks for coming so promptly." The Prime Minister entered the room with an aide.

"Sir there is something of great delicacy that Amelia and I need to discuss," said Hollinger, "alone."

The Prime Minister glanced at the Cabinet Secretary. Angus and the aide left without a word. They took seats opposite the PM in the middle of a large table with a green baize cover.

"Prime Minister...Simon, we have a serious fast developing situation that could escalate very quickly with catastrophic results that would endanger millions of lives. As you know Karl Orlov has demonstrated that he has infiltrated our nuclear power plants. Now he has demonstrated that he is also taken control over a highly important group of communications satellites. One of which is a strategic command and communications satellite used by the Ministry of Defence and NATO. He will be able to discover our capabilities and location of troops and assets."

"I can't believe I'm hearing this doesn't the MOD and NATO use encryption?"

"We use the very latest elliptical curve cryptography but there are a few flaws that need working on however he is one step ahead. We believe he has developed and deployed a new generation of quantum computing that is so powerful it can decrypt almost anything in near real time. Our view is based on the apparent ease that he can enter highly encrypted networks. We have had a communication from him demanding that Dr Graham and Professor Stanford are handed over to him."

"Where are they?"

Hollinger looked at his watch. "Well Elizabeth is half way across the Atlantic in a hypersonic jet. She should be arriving at Brize Norton within the next thirty minutes. She wanted to see her mother in Washington and Daniel is at Porton Down."

"Well you know government policy Anthony we don't give in to terrorist threats we just have to deal with it somehow. What would you advise?"

"My view is that at some point, whether it is now or days or weeks to come we will have no choice but to give him Elizabeth and we still don't know where the blighter is."

"Are you suggesting that we just hand her over? Surely that would just give him even more power."

"Yes with provisos. We have been working with scientists to produce a new communication tool using infra-sound. Scientists are already using infra-sound microphones to track herds of elephants in dense forests over huge distances. Many animals use infra sound, whales, hippos' even crocodiles. So it is possible to build into something like the heel of a shoe, an infra sound transmitter that will tell us precisely where Elizabeth's location is. Orlov will not have frequency scanners that will detect infra sound."

"And then what?"

"Simon this is so top secret even I'm not supposed to know about it. A very small group of scientists are working on a project that hasn't even been named yet and it could get us to Elizabeth but it's nowhere near ready for any kind of trials. So we need to play for time."

"How much time do we have?"

"I don't know, maybe a week or two. So we need delaying tactics and then when we do hand her over she has to stall as if her life depended on it, which it does."

"When we know Orlov's location can we not send in the SAS?"

"The Russians tried that in Kamchatka, absolute mayhem. He seems to have all manner of armed drones. We're developing anti-drone technology using lasers at Porton Down but they're a little behind because of budget cut backs."

"I'll speak to the Chancellor but what happens if this nameless project isn't built in time?"

"There is only one scenario left open to us."

Orlov was enjoying watching the progress of NATO manoeuvres in Sennelager in Northern Germany courtesy of Comsbird 4. Sennelager covering forty-five square miles, just to the north of Paderborn was the 20th Armoured Brigade Headquarters and Signal Squadron firing and training range. Type 56 Tank Regiment equipped with the 62 tonne Challenger 2 main battle tank, and two armoured infantry battalions frequently held exercises with NATO forces.

"I wonder how difficult it would be to patch into one of those big Challenger tanks," he mused.

Tapping on a flashing email, he opened the communication.

'Mr Orlov

We are urgently considering your request at the highest level. Doctor Graham and Professor Stanford are included in the on-going discussions. HM Government does not have the legal right or authority to compel either party to comply with your demand. In the event of them agreeing, assurances for their safety would have to be demonstrated. As you will appreciate this will take time and we would appreciate your patience.

Thank you.

Sir Anthony Hollinger

Director General of the SIS'

"My dear fellow, their security is my priority," said Orlov mockingly. "I'm afraid I'm going to have to concentrate your mind a little on the expediency of the matter in hand."

Elizabeth's flight touched down on the runway at Brize Norton safely and taxied over to its hanger. She was helped out of the hypersonic aircraft into a waiting helicopter that immediately took off for Porton Down. Inside the locker room she took off her flying suit and put on her own clothes just as Daniel arrived.

"I heard you got back Ok," he said with relief hugging her. "How's your mum taking all this?"

"She's taking it really well actually, seems to be quite friendly with a CIA agent or maybe I got that wrong. The G forces on the plane were ridiculous I was pinned to the seat and couldn't even lift my arms."

Hollinger came in. "Ah here you are," he said. "I've spoken with the Prime Minister. We've been formulating a plan but we need time for various projects to progress. Let's go over to the mess I'm sure you could do with some food and I could do with a drink."

The mess was quiet. A table in the corner was chosen for privacy.

"The plan is this. If you both decide to hand yourselves over to Orlov and there will be no pressure, it must be entirely your own decision, we have a method of tracking you that's 100% secure. Our people here are working on something quite extraordinary that could be used to get in and get you away from Orlov's base safely. I'm afraid I can't tell you any more than that. So the plan is to delay until Orlov becomes really impatient and then you go if you decide but you must drag out the work and think of everything you can to delay. The problem is there is no way of telling you when the cavalry is going to arrive, sorry. Oh did you enjoy your flight Elizabeth? I should have mentioned you're actually the first person to fly in a LAPCAT A3. You wouldn't catch me in one of these things, not a chance."

9

'I think our sensors need an overhaul,
there appears to be seismic activity
on the north-east coast of Scotland.'

Doctor Ian Smith's flight AirScotia AS041 from Vancouver touched down at Prestwick International Airport near Ayr, twenty minutes ahead of schedule. Passing through immigration was straight forward and he had to wait for his silver hard shell case to appear on the luggage conveyor belt and there was no one about in customs. He was already missing Alice and Josh but it was a year-long contract so he had made arrangements for them to follow once he had found a place to stay. He was looking forward to taking up his contract researching the effects of marine traffic on bottle nose dolphins. This was the first time he had worked for SAMS, based at Dunstaffnage Marine Laboratory on the Firth of Lorne near Oban in Scotland. Picking up the hire car he was soon travelling north-east towards Glasgow. Ian was thinking about Daniel and Elizabeth and that hair razing take off from the Kizimen Volcano. The hull actually ploughed a furrow through the edge of the rim before the sheer momentum of the seaplane broke it free. He had watched reruns of the violent volcanic explosions and since he hadn't heard from either of them, assumed they must have perished. He skilfully negotiated Glasgow's ring road and continued on through Clydebank, Dumbarton, passing Faslane where nuclear submarines were stationed towards some of the most spectacular scenery in the world. He stopped the car at a pub in Tarbet and bought haddock and chips, a half pint shandy then sat outside at a picnic table where the view was stunning. It was the magnificent backdrop of Ben Lomond reflected in the still dark waters of Loch Lomond. After lunch he continued his journey and eventually reached a large marina. Across the bay lay Dunstaffnage Marine Laboratory with the Castle further to the right on a promontory.

With its history of storms over the years the North Sea has always earned the respect of seasoned seafarers but the approaching storm that the TT Scandinavian an ultra large crude carrier (ULCC) was heading for was exceptionally powerful and only those onboard an oil supertanker of this size could feel relaxed. This was a newly built state of the art giant vessel with every conceivable electronic aid. On the deck it could be possible to fit 25 football pitches. The experienced fifty five year old Captain from Dhaka in Bangladesh looked at the white boiling sea a hundred feet below and marvelled that there was hardly a perceptible movement on the bridge. The stability was due to the 4,240,865 barrels of oil below. He had reduced the speed to eight knots because of the weather, half its capability. The vessel carried forty of a crew, thirty five Filipinos, three Indians and two from Bangladesh. Having taken on their cargo in Norwegian waters they were heading North around Scotland and then South for Argentina. At eighty feet her draught was too deep to safely negotiate the English Channel. The Captain was eating a plate of rice, spicy tempura fish and Dahl mopped up with Naan bread using his fingers in Bangladeshi custom while monitoring the instrument dials. The TT Scandinavian was on auto pilot and on schedule. He was listening to a weather warning on the radio predicting the storm force nine would strengthen to ten, just short of hurricane conditions. The captain stared at the compass and immediately saw that there was something wrong he looked at the stern and sure enough the vessel's wake was bending. They were changing course. He took the control off auto and set it to manual taking the helm. It did not respond and he could see that the ships' speed was increasing. He picked up the phone and spoke to the engine room but the engineer was locked out of the controls. The Captain studied his charts to see that they were heading straight for Scotland and the ship was reaching her maximum speed of sixteen knots. Some of the crew entered the bridge looking extremely puzzled and a little scared. The Captain decided to lower the huge rear anchors but there was no response he had lost control of the ship.

Angus McDonald the cabinet secretary to the prime Minister rushed into the cabinet office where the PM was meeting with the Chancellor of the Exchequer and departmental heads of the Treasury. He approached the PM and whispered in his ear.

The PM listened and said, "I'm sorry everyone, I have to curtail this meeting we'll reschedule it, my apologies."

Angus waited while they all trooped out. "Sir, I've just spoken with Sir Anthony Hollinger. He's on his way to give a fuller briefing. We have a serious situation developing in the North Sea. A May Day has been received from the TT Scandinavian; it's a massive oil tanker. The captain says that their computers are not responding and they have lost control of the ship."

Hollinger rushed into the cabinet office breathing heavily. "Simon this is potentially a maritime and landward disaster on a scale that we have never seen before. The Scandinavian is the latest flagship Ultra Large Crude Carrier (ULCC) in the world. Indeed it is the biggest moving construction ever built. It is a state of the art vessel relying heavily on computerized satellite navigation, imagery, depth monitoring, tracking and identifying ships in the vicinity and goodness knows what else. It is travelling at its maximum speed of sixteen knots. On its present course it is heading directly for the St Fergus Gas Terminal five miles North of Peterhead. The terminal is only 230 yards from the sea. St Fergus receives gas from twenty offshore platforms and supplies 20% of the UK's gas. This is the biggest of all the oil carriers. It takes five miles to go to a dead stop. She has a cargo capacity of over a half a million tons and is presently carrying 440,000 tons of highly combustible sweet crude oil."

Hollinger was sweating profusely and stopped for a moment to take a handkerchief out of his pocket to wipe his face.

"It has been calculated that the weight of the vessel and its speed means that even though St Fergus is protected by sand dunes the sheer energy created by the momentum of this giant ship will just keep going right through the centre of St Fergus."

Hollinger sat down red faced still sweating. "Can you just imagine the result if that happens? Ruptured gas pipes would ignite, shooting flames everywhere, hundreds of thousands of tons of oil pouring out all over the place would burn. The resulting explosions and burning oil would spread possibly reaching Peterhead to the South and Fraserburgh to the North, two of Scotland's major fishing towns. The impact on the North Sea environment and fisheries might take decades to recover. The MOD has dispatched four

Westland Sea King long range rescue helicopters to the area but the weather is awful. Six Euro-fighter Typhoon fighter jets have been scrambled from RAF Kinloss and HMS Vigilant a Vanguard-class submarine armed with Trident 2 D5 nuclear missiles is in the vicinity but will not reach the area in time."

Hollinger pressed at his tab and up came a map on the wall monitor showing the North-east of Scotland and the St Fergus Gas Terminal.

"How much time do we have Anthony?" asked the PM.

"Two hours and thirty two minutes. The RAF is briefed and waiting on a decision. The problem is the weather is so bad that it is unlikely that we will be able to get the crew safely off the vessel in time. Staff at St Fergus have set the shutting down process in motion and the offshore installations are shutting down production but that takes time and there will still be a lot of gas in the terminal."

"Anthony, I'm not a military man but can you answer me this. Assuming I decide to bomb the Scandinavian, what would it take short of a thermonuclear bomb to stop it?"

"I can't imagine that this scenario has ever been envisaged. I have no idea."

"Do you have someone with Dr Graham?"

"Yes. Justine Collingwood."

"I want to speak to her."

Elizabeth was in bed with Daniel when there was an urgent knock on the door. "Just a minute." She put on a dressing gown and opened the door.

"Sorry to disturb you Elizabeth but it's very important that you take this call," said Justine, handing her a mobile. "It's the Prime Minister."

"Hello."

"Elizabeth this is Simon Phillips, we have a very serious situation developing in the North Sea. I'm afraid Orlov is at it again. I think he has finally lost patience. There's an oil tanker bearing down on a gas terminal in Scotland and we're going to have to get Orlov to stop this thing happening. We don't have much time."

Elizabeth's face went white. She turned to Daniel who was sitting up in bed. "We have to see Orlov."

The prime minister heard her and rang off.

"Anthony how much time do we have now?"

"Two hours and four minutes," he replied.

"Send an email to Orlov. Tell him we'll comply with his request immediately. Get him to stop this tanker."

As Anthony was leaving the Cabinet Secretary came in.

"Angus has the Scottish Government been notified? The gas plant is in the process of shutting down and might not complete the process in time. Everybody in the area has to be evacuated immediately. Get me the First Minister."

Orlov was looking intently at a large screen. The image, supplied by a specialist optical surface mapping satellite was giving a simulation of the oil tankers progress towards the gas plant because the cloud-base was too low for conventional photography. He calculated that there was less than an hour until impact. His computer indicated that he had an email. He looked at the flashing icon and then back at the screen. They had plenty warning they should have evacuated the area by now. He regretted that the sea was too rough for lifeboats to be launched. He touched the email icon.

'Karl

Daniel and Elizabeth have agreed.

For pity's sake avert this disaster, you've won.

Give us your instructions.

Hollinger.'

He reached for a glass of champagne leaned back in his chair and putting his feet on the table swivelled the chair slightly to wait for the fireworks.

The whole crew of the Scandinavian assembled at the stern where two orange lifeboats were swinging from davits. Below a white foaming angry sea beckoned. The first lifeboat was lowered and released eight feet from the water and disappeared from view. It popped up a hundred yards from the stern of the ship. The second life boat began to lower and stopped fifteen feet from the water. Two crewmen with sharp knives one at each rope counted down from five, four, three, two, one then cut into the rope. The bow of the lifeboat dropped throwing out four of the men before the second rope snapped releasing the lifeboat that plunged under the water. By the time it came to the surface the Scandinavian was in the distance and another six seamen had disappeared. Two rescue helicopters appeared within minutes and as they were being winched up to safety they could see the burning St Fergus flare-stack glowing on the horizon.

The water was getting shallower and the ship started to slow down, fifteen knots, fourteen knots, ploughing a furrow in the soft sandy sea bed. Thirteen knots, her bow was lifting higher and higher dwarfing St Fergus, twelve knots and she had reached the perimeter fence, eleven knots and a fifth of her was on land still moving forward towering over the complex, ten knots and she struck the first layer of pipes. Then there was a massive explosion that ruptured the hull causing a wave of fire fanning out North, South and West. The stricken tanker was bathed in burning oil but continued until three quarters of the hull was on the land until it finally stopped. The other two processing plants hit by the wall of flame either side exploded, flames and smoke shooting thousands of feet in the air and as more fuel was released from the bow the sea behind went on fire. The fuel continued to leak pouring wave after wave of burning oil down towards Peterhead and up the coast towards Fraserburgh. The A90 to Aberdeen was gridlocked and similarly the A98.The explosions could be heard as far away as Aberdeen, Inverness and almost all the way up the Eastern Seaboard.

SBC TV channel's anchor woman stared in disbelief at her camera prompt.

"Police Scotland has just released a statement saying there has been a major incident at the St Fergus gas terminal in the North-East of Scotland involving a grounded oil tanker. Massive gas explosions are igniting hundreds of thousands of barrels of oil pouring from the stricken tanker. Emergency services are unable to get to the scene because of the intense heat and the burning oil is spreading towards Peterhead and Fraserburgh. These towns are being evacuated. Prime Minister Simon Phillips has declared a state of emergency and banned all civilian air traffic from the area. More than twenty offshore oil and gas producing platforms have shut down production. The coastguards and air sea rescue helicopters have picked up survivors believed to be crew members from the tanker. Our reporter Jocelyn McRae is live at Peterhead."

The light had faded quickly helped by the thick cloud. From a vantage point at Burnham on the South of Peterhead, the reporter stood exposed to the strong Easterly winds.

"Behind me the wall of flame from St Fergus has slowed down as it meets the River Ugie but incredibly it has still managed to cross the river and is threatening many houses. Some are already on fire and..."

There was a huge bang and gas flares and burning oil exploded spectacularly in the night sky to the North.

Jocelyn ducked. "...I am feeling the heat even at this distance and we have been advised that if the wind changes direction it could blow the deadly smoke this way, back to you in the studio."

"Thank you Jocelyn, stay safe. Environmentalists are claiming that although it is too early to be certain they believe that there will be minimal damage to fishing stocks in the North Sea due to the escaping oil being on fire."

'How many people dead?'

Orlov's email stared out of Hollinger's screen. "Maniac," he said.

'So far ten crewmen and many more on the mainland have been killed.'

'Regrettable, let's get down to business. Ensure that only Elizabeth and Daniel are at the

VIP Charter Lounge, Prestwick airport tomorrow at four pm.'

The First Minister of Scotland was furious. She was on the phone to Prime Minister Simon Phillips.

"This is absolutely unacceptable, why were we not told earlier? Exactly what is going on? I'm working in the dark here and I expect to have a full briefing. If Westminster is dealing with a terrorist threat and it affects Scotland it is only right for the Scottish Security Services to know in advance so that they can respond quickly and effectively. Prime minister, questions will be asked in the house. The economic, social and environmental impact of this attack on Scottish soil must be addressed."

The Prime Minister listened patiently. "I understand your concerns. We passed on information to the Scottish Government as soon as we received it. I will be making a statement to the house and rest assured we will continue until those responsible are held to account."

There was a low whistle followed by.

"Holy smoke, what the heck was that?"

The man was standing next to a bank of rolling graphs and monitors at the National Earthquake Information Centre in Denver Colorado. "Ben come and have a look at this." He said pointing at a graph. "I think our sensors need an overhaul, there appears to be seismic activity on the north-east coast of Scotland." The scanners were registering a three on the Richter scale.

"It doesn't make any sense that's not a seismically active area." Ben pressed a few buttons connecting to a data recording satellite in a geostationary orbit 500 miles above Scotland. "Yeah whatever it is has just been confirmed by our monitoring satellite. So our instrumentation's fine. I don't think I've come across anything quite like it."

The view of the Earth from the front port side of the international space station two hundred and sixty five miles up was spectacular as always. The Commander Gregor Andreyev never got tired of it. Northern Europe was in the dark. He took out his 18 X 50 image stabilized binoculars and marvelled at the twinkling lights of Paris and London. He took his eyes from the binoculars. Then he saw it a white flash followed by an intense red glow.

"Hey Mac take a look at this," he said.

Donald McLaren was doing the second of his twice daily exercises on the bike. He stopped and floated over to Gregor.

"What is it?" he asked.

"There's been a big explosion somewhere near Scotland."

"Bloody hell that's massive. Something that size could only be an oil platform or more likely a three oil platform complex. It's somewhere off the East of Scotland but there's too much cloud to tell. Whatever it is, for the light to penetrate that cloud it must be big."

Brian stood up and leaned against the rail. He looked across the line of other moored houseboats to the magnificent skyline of the City of San Francisco. A radio station playing easy listening music was coming inside through the half open window.

"Brian do you do this kind of thing all the time?" Ruby took a sip of beer from the bottle.

"What?"

"Protect people. I don't know, witness protection, safe houses, that kind of thing, do you?"

Brian thought for a moment, "I guess it is. Well, not all of the time but I'm usually called on when necessary."

"What kind of people do you protect?"

"All kinds of people for all kinds of reasons," he said evading the question.

"People like me?"

Brian was feeling a little uncomfortable and didn't want to go into detail. He smiled. "There are not many people like you Ruby. You know how it is, top secret." He tapped his nose."

Ruby took another sip and looked out over the Golden Gate Bridge. "You know all about me and I know next to nothing about you."

Brian sat down and took another sip. "Well I'm married sort of with three grown up children all boys who are making their way at various stages through college and it's costing me a fortune."

"Sort of?"

"What?"

"You said married sort of."

"I love my wife Ruby I just don't see her very often. Partly because of my job and partly because of her job, she's a community lawyer in Chicago. Goodness knows there's a lot of people there need her help." He reached over and put his arm around her. "I know it's against the rules but there's a really nice floating seafood restaurant not far from here."

"I think we may have already broken a few rules. One more won't hurt," she replied finishing her beer.

Inside, the music ended and a news bulletin began. "Forty-three people died when an oil tanker collided with a gas plant in Scotland and many more are missing. There was wide spread destruction of houses and crofts as fire swept through the countryside on a wave of burning oil caused by the running aground of the TT Scandinavian an ultra large crude carrier. This appears to be yet another terrorist attack on mainland Britain.

"Oh dear Brian these poor souls."

10

'Truth is in the mind of the beholder.'

The VIP charter lounge was quiet. Triple glazing cut out all the taxiing jet engine noises. It was separate from the main domestic terminal close to some large hangers. Elizabeth was looking out the window while Daniel poured out coffee into a pair of mugs.

"Just think Daniel, all of these horrible things happening because of me. People dying, oil and gas installations destroyed, this has to stop."

Daniel handed her a mug. "Orlov is crazy it's not your fault. I don't understand what he hopes to achieve, none of it makes any sense. Remember when he worked at the centre, he was the classic loner very secretive. I still don't know to this day what he was working on. He must have been able to access his own funding because he never asked me. After the balloon crash in Tanzania, Sonja the IT engineer tried to access his computer files and after several attempts it just died. So she took out the hard drive plugged it externally into her own but absolutely everything on it was heavily encrypted, she could do nothing with it."

Elizabeth put her head down. "I feel bad about the password," she said.

"What password?"

"For my laptop, I was angry. You probably didn't hear me tell Orlov. I saw Jani leaving the office. Do you remember there was a loud bang when we were walking away through the forest in Kamchatka?"

Daniel drank the black coffee and put his mug down. He gave Elizabeth a hug.

"Jani was no saint have you forgotten what happened, she kidnapped you?"

Elizabeth gave a wry smile. "It doesn't help," she said.

The door opened and with that, a howl of jet engines from outside pierced the silence. Standing there backlit was the unmistakable outline of Jani. She was smiling but not in a nice way. She turned and led the way. A pilotless small jet in black livery with a gold painted horizontal line running along the fuselage and diagonally up the tail was waiting. The engines were turning as they climbed the steps. Elizabeth recognized the inside, everything was white. She and Daniel sat next to each other with a table in front of them. Jani closed the door and sat at the other side of the table, her gazed fixed on Elizabeth. Within seconds the aircraft's jets pointing down took off vertically and then with a roar swivelled to the rear and headed west out to sea.

"I'm glad you're Ok Jani," said Elizabeth. "Really, I had a suspicion that there might be a bomb in the laptop but only a suspicion. If it's any consolation it was intended for me."

Jani looked out of the window. "The way you reacted to it made me suspicious. So I used a bomb proof bag. They're standard issue at most airports now."

"Jani, what's Karl going to do, he says he's going to save the world?" asked Daniel.

"Karl is a genius. If he says he is going to save the world I would imagine that's exactly what he's going to do."

"Yes but how?" asked Elizabeth.

"I have no idea. Perhaps it's a dream, perhaps he's serious sometimes it's hard to tell. I never ask Karl anything but whichever way, if he is serious it will work."

Hollinger was sitting at a computer monitor, one of a bank of six with an analyst. The infra sound locater was pulsing a dot on a map.

"That's strange," said the analyst. "The transponder is giving a location reading, the infra sound is confirming that location but there is no radar shadow."

"What does that mean?" asked Hollinger.

"Well at the moment they are leaving air traffic control space two hundred miles off the coast of Scotland on a heading 225 degrees south-west out in the Atlantic. If they happen to switch off the transponder..." Before he could finish the sentence the transponder stopped transmitting. "...Ah we wouldn't be able to locate them without the IF tracker."

"Can we use HawkSat's stealth tracker? "Just in case we lose the IS signal," said Hollinger.

"Sorry sir it's been priority commandeered."

They watched the tracker marker's steady pulse changing course to a bearing of 026 degrees.

"If they continue on that course where will it take them?" asked Hollinger sitting on the edge of his seat.

The analyst brought up another screen and enlarged it to show the west coast of Scotland.

"It looks like they are heading for a small group of islands off Scotland near the coast of South Uist."

The tide was well up on Dornabay beach. The jet slowed down and the engines swivelled bringing the aircraft to a hover. They watched out the window as the beach disappeared in a cloud of sea spray from the down thrusting jets making a slowly descent. It was a perfect vertical landing manoeuvre on the wet beach. It taxied up the ramp as the hanger doors opened and the engines shut down. Jani opened the door and lowered the steps climbing down followed by Elizabeth and Daniel. She attached the winch to the aircraft and it started to move into the hanger. The hanger door closed and lights came on. Waiting for them was Orlov with a broad smile.

"Got them," Hollinger whooped thumping the table, jiggling the screens. The blip disappeared from the screen.

"Let's see if we can get an ultra-high resolution drone over the island. What's it called, Dornabay?"

He picked up the phone and dialled the number for Brize Norton.

"We've been through a lot, the four of us." Orlov was pouring drinks from a decanter into glasses on a tray. "I am so glad to see you again, and I have to admit, I didn't think I would."

"You're a maniac Karl you have to stop killing people," said Elizabeth.

He put the tray of glasses onto the coffee table and helped himself to one sitting down. "I don't like collateral damage you know that Elizabeth but I wasn't being taken seriously and that dreadful man Hollinger tipped off my fellow countrymen and as you saw they paid us a visit. He could have killed you two as well by the way. Once my location was known well that was that. I had to destroy it, sad. And Daniel did you have to let SIS know I could enter their network, tut, tut." He took a sip from his glass.

"What do expect, you tried to kill me with a drone. What's going on Karl what's the plan?" Daniel looked intently at Orlov.

They were in an identically laid out building to the one in Kamchatka, almost an exact copy in fact. The only difference was that in place of the window overlooking the forest, a massive screen along the entire wall was showing an 8K resolution video image of the beach.

"Plan." He replied flatly, folding his arms. "Sorry, I'm not quite with you."

"Well is it the world domination thingy you know like James Bond villains? Which one are you? Hugo Drax, Goldfinger, Blofeld?"

Orlov laughed out loud. "Choose your next witticism carefully professor it may be your last." He said unfolding his arms. "World domination, dear me no I don't want to dominate the world I want to save the world." Orlov stood up and walked to a table that had a bowl of fruit. Picking up an orange he leant against the table holding it out for inspection. "There are many different species of parasites on this wonderful planet of ours that engage with their hosts in different ways, but the objective is always the same. To replicate, they must feed on their hosts. Viruses, bacteria, insects, fungus, even cuckoos parasitize. But there is only one parasitic species that can kill the host without benefit to themselves and thereby ending their existence, the human species." He tossed the orange up in the air and caught it. "The host is the world we live in." He said putting it back in the bowl. "There is no accurate way to calculate the exact population of the world because it's so dynamic, births, deaths happening all the time but the nearest we can get to it is approximately 7.3 billion. That's seven thousand three hundred million people. Accounting for deaths, the world's population is growing at 100 million a year. And as the population grows its growth becomes exponential, so, what to do? Is the quantity of life more important than the quality of life? I don't think so." Orlov sat down.

Elizabeth frowned. "Well we have to hope that a reduction of child mortality, an increase in living standards, access to food and fresh water will give parents hope and encourage smaller families," she said.

"Mm, do you think? Noble sentiment I'm sure, however by the time that does or does not happen it will be too late. Changing the subject slightly though it is related, I have been working on a bio accelerated nano quantum processor with 3d architectured solid state memory. The outside world believes that the fastest computer is in Guangzhou in China. It has 3,120,000 cores. I call that brute force computing. The term artificial intelligence is somewhat derogatory and as such generates fear but given the correct parameters is perfectly safe. I prefer to call it intelligent agents. So I have developed an intelligent agent, a biotech hybrid computer, infinitely more powerful than any existing computer and it's based on the Neurosynaptic Chip principle. Scaled down versions could be small enough to put onto your wrist or grafted into a brain. Isn't it curious that the anticipation of pain can be worse than pain itself, reducing the painfulness and yet the anticipation of pleasure can heighten the pleasured? There's someone I'd like you to meet. Come with me."

They entered the elevator and seconds later the door slid open revealing a gallery and thirty feet below was an oval pool. The clear water was slowly moving and undulating but there was no sign of the bottom. Orlov reached over and hit a large button on the wall. A door slid open from the wall of the pool and a small shark swam in with its triangular fin above the water. Disorientated it swam in circles. From the deep a large shape got bigger and clearer and then a massive octopus burst from the water.

"Meet Saskia." He said with a hint of pride. "She is Enteroctopus dofleini, the Giant Pacific Octopus."

The shark thrashed about but eight massive sucker covered arms enveloping it pulling it closer and closer to her huge sharp beak. The bulbous head with an eye either side was covered with dermal rippling skin that changed colour mimicking the pooling of the shark's red blood. Eventually it stopped struggling and the octopus sank disappearing into the depth of the pool with its prey. Elizabeth and Daniel held each other in shock at the unexpected violence they had witnessed.

"She's twenty feet across and weighs a hundred pounds at least that was what she was when I checked her last. She has 2,240 suction cups so once she has a hold nothing can break free. Her method of killing is honed by the passage of hundreds of millions of years in evolutionary design. She injects compounds with her bite that paralyse its prey then she digests it at her leisure. Fascinating isn't she?"

Elizabeth was aware that Daniel was shaking and squeezed his hand. "Yes but why the cabaret and what's the next act?" he said angrily.

"Do calm yourself Daniel you'll do yourself an injury. Octopuses are very clever. Scientists are just beginning to measure their IQ. Saskia is a donor my impatient friend, supplying stem cells from her sizeable brain for my little project which, I have to say, is progressing very well. As the stem cells grow, there will be a mutual interaction between the growing brain and the computer. In effect they will become one. A truly, thinking, self-aware, highly intelligent agent." Orlov paused for effect. "I call her Alatheia, the Goddess of Truth. Like beauty, truth is in the mind of the beholder."

Doctor Ian Smith was piloting the marine research catamaran Pathfinder III south of Barra. Ten metres in length it was the smallest of Dunstaffnage's research vessels. The cabin space was surprisingly generous with an en suite bedroom, a galley and living space, a wet lab, computer lab and workshop. The computerized wind sensor sails were GPS linked needing very little input from him. The wind filled the mainsail and jib as it rounded the north headland of Mingulay. Mingulay, Berneray and Pabbay owned by the National Trust for Scotland were remote and lonely places where only wildlife lived. He loved this job and he particularly liked being alone in such places. Rhona and Josh had arrived and were staying in a nice cottage near a small beach north of Oban. He would see them both again in a few days when he got back. He was trailing a weighted underwater microphone attached to recording equipment hence the need for a sail boat. Half way between Pabbay and Dornabay, he dropped sail and set anchor. There was enough of a swell to give a pleasant motion to the boat. It was about six in the evening and time for a beer. He opened the cooler took one out flipping off the cap. Holding one of the headphones against an ear he sat back in his chair on the deck and sipped from the bottle. He moved forward to the fixed table quickly where his audio equipment was laid out and pressed record. Faint sounds were coming through the headphone. Then a burst of rapid clicking sounds changing in frequency, then another and another. Ian thought that this wasn't just communicating it could almost be described as duetting. He put down his beer, fixed the headphones to both ears leaned back enjoying the sounds and closed his eyes. Then they died away. Ian opened his eyes to see something metallic glinting in the clear early evening sky. He took off the head phones and picked up a pair of binoculars. Yes there was something very high up. It was a strange looking aircraft.

Hollinger stared at the images of Dornabay on his screen. There was nothing, not even sheep. All it had was scrub vegetation and wind stunted dwarf trees.

"I don't get it," he said. "Could they have been forced to dump their clothing and shoes from the aircraft?"

"It's possible," said the analyst.

"Widen out." The island got smaller. "What's that, a boat? Zoom in on it please."

The catamaran filled the screen showing Ian looking at the drone through binoculars. He put the binoculars down and picked up his beer.

"Is face recognition scanning?" A square box locked on to Ian's face and up came a picture of him in a separate screen. "I do not believe it. I do not believe it. What on earth is he doing here? Doctor Ian Gerard Smith our friend from Vancouver." Hollinger took off his glasses and rubbed his eyes.

He started to laugh. The analyst looked at him in surprise. He had never heard so much as a chuckle from the Director General of the SIS. Hollinger shook his head and took a handkerchief from his pocket to clean his glasses.

"Oh dear," he said. "Whatever next, should I bring him in, I wonder?"

A yellow alert flashed on Orlov's monitor coming from the drone-skimmers. He tapped the screen on his holoband and up came the distant image of Ian's catamaran. "What do we have here?" he asked. Circling an icon the image enlarged showing Ian on deck drinking a beer. Daniel stared transfixed with disbelief.

"Looks harmless," said Orlov then pressed stand down.

Daniel glanced at Elizabeth who was unaware of the drama. They hadn't recognised Ian because of his recently grown beard. Orlov got up and touched Jani's shoulder.

"Jani can you go to the holding tank and ensure that Saskia's meals are well fed? Thank you." Jani obediently left. "As we speak, Alatheia is busy compiling a computer model of the world. Geology, geography, topography, weather systems, population dynamics, economics, the list is almost endless. When it is complete there will be rational logical and preferably pain free answers to questions that the world's leaders are incapable of addressing. Alatheia will supply holistic solutions based on an understanding of the complexity of our planet that no human can. Non-specifically the plan as you call it would be to reduce the populace to sustainable economic and environmental levels. There is not a single problem in the world that cannot be solved by a reduction in the population. The question is not what to do but how to do it. Timescale is important. Global warming will reach tipping point within the next few years and then it's irreversible. Ice caps are melting, the oceans are getting saltier and sea levels are rising."

"Karl, I don't understand. When you studied at the NRC you were objectionable in an almost likeable way but what happened to change you so much or were you always a Jekyll and Hyde?"

"I'm still the same person it's the world that's changing. East Africa opened my eyes, the cities teeming with people barely able to survive. When we were plunging to earth in that burning balloon I made a promise to God, yes to God that if I survived I would find a way to end the suffering. The ballooning accident was an opportunity to disappear. I made the mistake of asking for favours in Moscow to fund my research. I wanted to be independent of the NRC establishment instead I became dependent on another establishment so I had to very quickly learn to bend the rules until they broke. It is never possible to pay back those kinds of favours. That's the name of the game. It's called ownership. So I went from breaking the rules to breaking the law it's an easy step to take really. You know Elizabeth this is all irrelevant, what is important is this, will the world survive with its increasing population?"

What are you suggesting?" asked Elizabeth, "compulsory euthanasia?"

"We're almost on the same page and I'm open to suggestions but that sounds a little clumsy," He replied.

"What does all this have to do with me and Remembrance?"

"As I mentioned before it would greatly benefit me if a number of my enemies had a sudden and inexplicable loss of memory."

"Well I haven't perfected it yet. I can access memory but I have not deleted any. It is a theoretical possibility yes, but that's not a guarantee. Anyway wasn't it destroyed in Kamchatka?"

"Yes, I couldn't save the one you worked on in Russia in time but I backed up the Langley copy of Remembrance on Alatheia.

"So were back to square one?"

"Precisely. The interior of my home is exactly the same as in Russia. You will find everything you need here. Daniel once again you will be Elizabeth's primate."

Ruby and Brian were in bed. There was a gentle motion from a passing tug boat. Patterns of moving dappled light on the ceiling were reflections off the rippling water from the street lamps. They changed and dissolved into each other.

"Are you sleeping?" Ruby whispered.

"Yes." said Brian.

"I'm worried about Elizabeth."

"I know."

"Don't they tell you anything?"

"Elizabeth is somewhere in Scotland. That's all I know."

"Is she with Daniel?"

"Yes, and that's all I know."

"Are they Ok?"

"Yes and that really is all I know."

"Thank you."

They turned over and held each other. Ruby's tears rolled down her cheeks and touched Brian.

"It'll be Ok you'll see," he said.

The full moon had started to wane and hung low on the horizon. Ian was stir frying mackerel he had caught earlier with carrots, red pepper, courgettes, sweet corn, 2 medium eggs and a tablespoon of light soy sauce with a dash of Prosecco. The moon was casting enough light for him to cook without switching the lights on. Above and unnoticed Perseids meteor shower was raining across the night sky. Ian left the stir fry bubbling away and stepped out of the cabin. He was more interested in little flecks of light in the sea. Lying face down on the deck he put his fingers into the water. The slack tide was beginning to turn, moving between his fingers. Phosphorescent Corophium, a type of small shrimp reacted to his fingers and sparkled. Fish swam by leaving trails of ghostly green light. He was in paradise. What more could he want and yet he felt guilty. Here he was enjoying life while two good friends had perished. He tuned in the radio as he ate the stir fry. Speculation by the media that it was a terrorist attack on the Scottish mainland was increasing. Reports concluded that since all of the offshore gas fields had switched off supply to St Fergus it had reduced the intensity of the fire and there would be an attempt to use controlled explosives to extinguish the blazing oil. Ian switched off the radio, regretting he had turned it on. He put his plate down and leaned back in his chair seeing for the first time the meteor shower.

The firing started but before the bullets reached the target it was enveloped in bluey green swirling plasma. As the firing stopped the plasma disappeared revealing an untouched mannequin.

The soldiers and scientists at the covered floodlit firing range at Porton Down checked with binoculars. A soldier picked up a laser guided RPG shoulder launcher and fired it. This time the target was an old Landrover fitted with the same equipment. Once again the plasma appeared instantly but this time the grenade exploded way behind the target. The Landrover was untouched.

"You missed." The group laughed.

"This baby never misses."

It worked. This was the nameless invention that Hollinger had been talking about. Using a shield of heated plasma and alternating frequency short range lasers. It deflected the bullets and missiles by bending them around the target. The idea of the alternating frequencies came from the wild. Giant lemurs in Madagascar use non-synchronous alternating sound frequencies off pitch to scare away their only natural predator, the Fosse.

"Morning Amelia can you send me the file on Dr Ian Smith please." Hollinger didn't have to wait long before it showed up on his screen. "What could be better cover than reality?" he thought as Ian's mobile number showed up on a list of personal details.

Ian had his headphones on listening to all the various underwater sounds while eating some instant porridge. He had slept in after the late night and was busy trying to catch up when the mobile phone in his shirt pocket vibrated. He took of the headphones and looked at the unfamiliar number.

"Hello?"

"Dr Smith?"

"Yes?"

"My name is Sir Anthony Hollinger and I'm the Director General of the Secret Intelligence Service in London."

Ian put down his bowl. A dribble of porridge stuck to his unkempt brown beard.

"I have some news for you. Professor Stanford and Dr Graham are very much alive."

"What? That's incredible but I saw the news pictures, nobody could have survived the volcano. That's where I left the Kolb."

Ian was in shock. Having experienced losing a good friend and now being told that they were safe was hard to comprehend.

"Well incredible might be the wrong word, I would think miraculous would be more suitable but they are still in danger. Orlov whom I believe you know also survived. We would very much like you to help us. But firstly I am not a great believer in coincidence can you tell me how you happen to be in this part of the world?"

"I'm a marine biologist on a years' contract working out of Dunstaffnage near Oban. This was planned quite some time ago, why?"

"Orlov has moved his base to Scotland. If you look at the small island astern, called Dornabay, that is the last trace we have of the pair. We would very much like you to continue your work but a little closer to the island and report back on this number if you see anything unusual."

"But there's nothing on it, not even sheep."

"It's our only hope of finding them. Please keep this information to yourself otherwise it may compromise any rescue attempt, goodbye."

Ian looked at his phone wondering if he had just imagined the conversation.

"Ruby, I've just had a call. I have to leave right away. There'll be an agent arriving soon," said Brian starting to packing.

Ruby's face crumpled.

"It's Jean, my wife. She's been in a car accident. They've taken her to the Mercy Hospital and Medical Centre in Chicago. It's very serious."

"Oh I'm so sorry Brian."

A car pulled up at the pier and Brian awkwardly kissed Ruby on the cheek. "Ruby this is Jane Seymour. Jane has been fully briefed and she will be with you until I'm back."

"Pleased to meet you Ma'am," she said. Agent Seymour handed over the keys and shook Ruby's hand as over her shoulder Brian was already walking away along the pier.

"Daniel, have you ever had anything bad happen in your life that still bothers you?"

Daniel looked at Elizabeth but she avoided his gaze preferring to keep working on the computer.

"Well that's easy. When I was a small boy I fell asleep in my uncle's barn. Hay had been freshly cut that day and the smell was wonderful I can still remember what that was like. When I woke up a large spider was chewing my leg. It left a raw bleeding wound that took a couple of months for it to heal and I still have the scar."

"You never told me. So that's why you don't like spiders. Do you remember how old you were?"

"I was ten. I was on my uncle's farm in the South Hams and it was his birthday. Let's see the thirtieth no the thirty-first of July 1993, late morning.

"Remembrance is practically up and working with a few minor adjustments, I haven't told Karl yet. Would you like me to get rid of your arachnophobia?"

Daniel nodded.

11

'What's that?'

'What?'

'There.'

'That's Ol Donyo Lengaï, the mountain of God.'

The boomerang twisted through the air spinning as it returned to its owner when it was caught in mid-air by a border collie.

"Trigger," said a child's voice in exasperation.

Elizabeth was watching Daniel on the monitor and listening on a pair of headphones hearing the ten year old boy calling.

"Leave it."

The dog came up tail wagging to return the boomerang. Daniel threw it again but this time he ran to hide from Trigger in the barn. It was dark. Daniel climbed high up over large square bales of hay until he could touch the corrugated roof. He lay down peeking over the edge to see if Trigger would find him. With no sign of the dog Daniel turned over and within seconds his eyes closed. Elizabeth put a start marker on the time line and ran the clock forward until Daniels eyes opened again. He looked at his knee to see a large spider feeding on a wound. Daniel screamed and brushed the spider away. He jumped down from the bales running screaming into the farmhouse kitchen where a man was sitting at a wooden table drinking tea from a large mug and reading a paper.

"Uncle Peter I've been bitten by a spider."

The knee was looking angry and had started bleeding.

"It looks sore I have just the thing right here." He reached up to a shelf and took down an old tin box and put it on the table. "Let's see." He fished around and took out a tube of cream.

"Am I going to die?" asked Daniel.

Uncle Peter looked very serious. "You're not going to die Dan," he said applying the cream. "In any case your mother would kill me if you did. There, now just forget about it and it'll soon clear up. Are you ready for something to eat?"

Elizabeth put an end marker on the timeline and stopped the clock. She glanced at Daniel whose eyes were closed and looked at the keyboard. Her fingers moved hovering over the keyboard hesitated and then withdrew. She looked at Dan again, braced herself, typed on the keyboard and then pressed enter. There was a slight shudder from Daniel. Elizabeth turned the clock back to just before the start marker and started the clock. She could see Daniel climbing up the bales, waiting for the dog then turning over, eyes closing and after a few seconds.

"Are you ready for something to eat?"

Elizabeth took off the headphones and stopped the clock. She closed her eyes and breathed a sigh of relief. She powered down the program took off Daniels' latex helmet and decided to let him sleep off the mild anaesthetic.

"Now where can I find a spider?" she thought.

Orlov was alone in his office. He tapped on a panel on the door locking him in. He activated Holovue and touched several icons. The screen changed from an image of the sea to a large circular glass domed room. A swirling opalescent egg shaped creature that was Alatheia gently floated as if suspended above a circular table covered with a blue gel-like material.

"Hello Karl," she said.

"Alatheia can I have a progress report on Virtual Earth," he asked.

Layers of light streamed down from the dome to meet the surface of the table forming one huge hologram of the world. Multiple images had been harnessed and combined seamlessly giving the earth an extraordinary depth of detail. It was like viewing from a space station but with a great deal more clarity. Orlov watched as the hologram slowly revolved. The vast Pacific Ocean, America then Africa was vivid with the spectacular resolution as he zoomed in.

"What are the main problems affecting Planet Earth and how can they be resolved?" he asked.

"At a western standard of living, planet earth's resources can only sustain 2 billion people. That means reducing the present population by 5.3 billion. As

Planet Earth's resources are used the sustainable levels of population will also be reduced."

"Alatheia please show the order of countries using most to least resource consumers per capita."

"Black is the highest to white the lowest."

Orlov kept watching. The highest consumers of resources were in the richest parts of the world, Oceania, North America, Europe, Latin America, Asia and lastly Africa. But the poorest parts of the world had the highest numbers of people. China, India, United States, Indonesia, Brazil. Only the USA was high on both lists.

"What would be the most humane method of reducing populations?"

"There is no humane way to reduce population sizes in time to avoid irrevocable damage to planet earth."

"What would you suggest?"

"I suggest a targeted release of a hybrid pheromone borne bacterium-virus that will discriminate between population densities, ages, sexes and ethnicity killing five out of seven people on Planet Earth. The virus is infectious transmitted from person to person during the release of human modulator pheromones. It is sleep inducing and painless resulting in a coma and death. There will be an undetectable incubation period of thirty days with no symptoms. This is as humane as is possible."

"Can you do that?" said Orlov.

"Yes. Do you wish me to proceed?"

"Yes," he said. "I most certainly do and I will need an antidote."

Sausalito's Galilee harbour in Marin County had quite a large community of houseboats. From the land they just looked like a motley collection of odd looking wooden houses. Some were modest and anonymous like Ruby's others had style and stood apart. One even had a grand piano. Ruby was drying some dishes and agent Seymour was outside taking a call. She spent a lot of time on the phone or texting. Ruby was missing Brian. Jane came inside looking sombre.

"I've just heard from Brian, sadly his wife didn't recover from the accident. The funeral's tomorrow."

"Oh dear," said Ruby, "poor Brian."

Hollinger was in the Hashiguchi sushi bar with his wife Mary chewing on a mouthful of sashimi when his mobile phone rang out. The sound of a woodpecker emerged from his pocket.

"Hello."

"Hollinger, its Ian Smith."

"Dr Smith," he mumbled picking up a glass of saké. "Just a moment." Hollinger got up. "I'm sorry dear I won't be long." Mary gave him a look as he walked out onto the street. "What news?" he asked.

"Well I've been all around Dornabay and there is a slip but it doesn't seem to go anywhere. There are also some strange looking things in rock pools dotted round the island."

"What are they like?"

"Like upside down woks on spidery legs. I'm sorry I can't think of any other way to describe them."

"Upside down what?"

"Woks, you know frying pans."

"Oh, thank you Dr Smith, You've been most helpful. Stay well back from the island but keep it in view. Thank you again." Hollinger went back inside and sat down.

"You really ought to change that ringtone," she said.

"I can't. Your son Alex put it on. It's the coolest ringtone around apparently and I don't know how to change it."

"He's your son too," she said smiling.

Elizabeth was watching the detailed image of the sea shore on the wall screen. It really did feel like looking out of a window. The ultra-high resolution camera was fixed just above the flat mossy bank. Waders began to fly in to their high tide roost. Elizabeth watched mesmerized by the sheer numbers of different species, redshank, oystercatcher, turnstone, and greenshank arriving in a blizzard of wings with curlews and the odd whimbrel, late arrivals. They would stay until the waters receded and then they could start feeding, following the dropping tide all over again. A natural cycle that's as endless as time itself. They stood on one leg with the other tucked into their downy feathers facing into the wind. Heads turned and bills buried under the feathers on their backs. Some with eyes open some closed, they would swivel on one leg as the wind veered.

"It's not Boris but it's still a wonderful sight."

Orlov had just entered the room with Jani who walked over to get a closer look.

"Truly amazing," said Elizabeth. "Karl I was thinking, do you and Jani have any long term effects from the ballooning accident?"

Jani turned to Elizabeth. "Yes," she said. "There's not a night I don't waken in a sweat with flashbacks, why?"

Elizabeth looked at Orlov. "Because my dear, Elizabeth wants to experiment on us," he said

"No I don't need to, it works. I did a test on Daniel."

"You don't think I'd be foolish enough to allow you to poke around inside my memory, you could delete anything and everything," said Orlov.

Elizabeth shrugged her shoulders and turned back to watch the waders hopping about on one leg. Jani went over to Orlov and put her arms round his waist and whispered in his ear.

"But if Jani wishes it I would be willing for you, under my supervision of course, to delete her memories from that day."

The three went to Elizabeth's lab where Daniel was having a snooze.

"Come on Dan wakeup." Elizabeth turned to see Jani smile and kiss Orlov on the cheek.

"I hope you're not squeamish Elizabeth, it will not be pleasant viewing."

Daniel got up and Jani lay down. "I'll need the time and dates," she said.

Elizabeth gave Jani a mild sedative injection. She entered a date and time and put on the headphones. The image burst on to the screen of a crowd looking up at Jani from the ground. She set a start marker. The ground fell away beneath them and the people waved getting smaller and smaller as the gas burner roared pumping more hot air into the balloon. Orlov and Daniel watched pensively not knowing how they would react. Elizabeth had a slight attack of motion sickness and steadied herself against Daniel who was standing behind. She had forgotten how good looking Karl was and she could see right away, he was in love. His face was alive with a huge grin and his eyes sparkled. The guide was busy scoping with binoculars and photographing constantly. The balloon travelled along a gorge in the Gol Mountains. Scores of Rupels Griffon Vultures with huge wingspans left their nesting colonies as the balloon approached catching a lift from localized thermals coming from the plains and flew round the balloon basket.

"*This is fantastic,*" said Jani hugging Karl.

It was like a scene from a primordial movie on dinosaurs. They were heading towards the vast plains of the Serengeti.

"What's that?" Asked Jani.

"What?"

"There."

"That's Ol Donyo Lengaï, the mountain of God."

"It's smoking."

"It's an old dormant volcano."

"What's that, pink stuff on Lake Natron?"

"They're Flamingos."

The deep, deep blue of Natron with fluttering pink dots grew bigger as they dropped height. The conical shape of Ol Donyo Lengaï had drifting clouds of steaming fumaroles. Then they were crossing the plains overtaking hundreds of thousands of migrating animals. Ribbons of animals crossing rivers were caught by waiting crocodiles snapping at their legs. Zebras and Wildebeest scrambled up the river banks as the crocs pulled the unlucky victims into the water leaving floating dead animals drifting downstream. Up again and across the plains where animals were grazing peacefully until Karl set the burner roaring and the animals began to run, only this time he couldn't shut the burner off. They were gaining height too quickly so he pulled the cords to spill the hot air from the envelope. Then the balloon caught fire plunging rapidly down twisting as it went with huge sheets of flaming material raining down on the three of them. Everything including the wicker basket the guide, Orlov and Jani were on fire. They were screaming with fear and pain. Orlov looked away from the monitor and Elizabeth pulled off the headphones with a mixture of horror and tears. She reached forward and speeded up the clock. The screen went blank when Jani passed out. Elisabeth set an end marker and made a few quick calculations.

She looked at Orlov who had a hand over his brow, and pressed enter. Then she powered down the computer. The tension in the room was intense.

"Thank you Elizabeth," said Karl quietly.

12

'Nine million passengers pass through
Heathrow and Gatwick airports every month.'

Dr Ian Smith was on his last beer. Reluctantly he took it out of the small cool-box flipped off the cap and drank some. It had been a long afternoon. He decided another half an hour and he would pack it in. He put the headphones back on and relaxed in his chair. There were a series of boyng sounds getting closer and he wrote in his ledger the time, date location and the species, Minke Whale. It broke the surface close to Ian's boat and exhaled a shower of hot air and water. Ian managed to get a photograph before it disappeared. It was almost as though it had popped up to take a look at the catamaran. Ian sat down again. It was peaceful and unusually still. He was thinking it wouldn't be long before he would be home with Rhona and Josh. Then a distant almost imperceptible sound caught his attention. It was a very faint irregular throbbing sound. Where had he heard that before? It got louder and more regular. He smiled to himself, of course. He was hearing the propeller and pump sounds that a nuclear submarine makes when travelling through water. He scanned with his binoculars just in time to see a trail of what could have be an optical mast disappearing underwater. The sounds faded. Did he imagine it? Perhaps he shouldn't spend so much time on his own after this.

Sharp and Hollinger linked up to a securely encrypted conference link. Murray Greig from the MOD started the meeting.

"Sir Anthony the Astute class submarine HMS Axiom is in position off Dornabay. And we have some very old records held by the Scottish Government that show that an extensive connection of underground bunkers on the island is capable of withstanding a nuclear explosion. Dr Smith is still in the area by the way. There are twelve crack specialist SAS commandos equipped with the very latest pieces of kit, six Plasma Laser protected low profile surface

XSR Interceptor speedboats. They can safely mount an attack on the island when required to."

Hollinger peered at the screen. "Orlov has a defence ring round the island, water skimming drones it seems. I'm assuming that this device has been thoroughly tested, but even so I don't think I'd be too confident. Orlov is a very resourceful man and we still don't know what his game plan is."

Sharp put on her glasses and looked down at some notes. "It is impossible to track his online movements. He seems to be using a string of self-made VPNs so I'm afraid we're very much in the dark. This was the last location from the infra-sound transmitter and it stopped soon after it arrived here. It wouldn't be able to transmit through blast proof doors meant to defend against a nuclear attack. What should our next move be?"

"I think the PM should be informed."

The PM was startled. "Are you suggesting detonating a thermonuclear device on Dornabay?"

"If we have ground penetrating capability we'll need only one. This is an extremely dangerous man he needs to be stopped," said Hollinger.

The Prime Minister took off his glasses and closed his eyes. "Don't be ridiculous Anthony, no. There is no scenario that I can, in my wildest dreams, ever imagine that would cause me to explode a nuclear device in Scotland. I doubt whether the First Minister would think it was appropriate. We'll just have to wait. We have very little options open. He'll get careless and make a move and then we'll have him."

Orlov was dressed in a yellow Biohazard suit Certified to NFPA 1994, the Standard for First Responders to Chemical, Biological, Radioactive, and Nuclear protective ensembles. He was in a room containing two large seal-able 3D printers with glass fronts. One was busy creating the last of seven metal canisters. The other loaded with a file from Alatheia was ready to print a complex mix of nano particle chemicals and protein. It had created a synthetic hybrid virus unknown to the human species. With a highly contagious incubation period it targets the brain causing subarachnoid haemorrhaging, fatigue and death. The long incubation period would ensure that by the time the High Security Infectious Disease Unit at the Royal Free Hospital in London was alerted it would be too late for any isolation strategies. In the process of dying with the host, the virus would alter becoming inert.

The printer pinged indicating that the canister inside was full. This was the dangerous part. Orlov opened the door, tightened a valve and slowly and gently detached the nozzle on the canister taking it out of the printer. He attached a Wi-Fi controlled servo motor to the valve. The canister had a label saying;

'Intake Air Handling Unit cleaner.'

Orlov went through a decontamination shower just in case of any leaks, removed his suit and returned to his office. He hacked into Heathrow's Procurement Department in Glasgow and issued an Isupplier order number to a non-existent company with instructions to service the five air intake towers. He made a similar order with Gatwick's Procurement team to service two air intake towers. He issued and downloaded security cleared identity documents. Leaving the dates of service open-ended he retreated from their servers without leaving a trace. Everything was in place. Jani came in and put her arms around his neck kissing him on the top of the head. She was more like the Jani before the accident since Elizabeth had deleted it from her memory, carefree, girly and frivolous. He had got his Jani back. When all this was over maybe he and Jani would go back in a year's time to East Africa, probably Tanzania.

"What is it that you're doing?" she asked.

"Do you trust me Jani?"

"Of course, if it wasn't for you I'd be dead."

"You saved my life too," he said picking up a white leather briefcase from below the table. He took out two hypo syringes that were both filled with a liquid.

"This will give us a great deal of protection," he said injecting himself.

"What is it?" she asked.

"This is where you have to trust me." Jani immediately offered her arm.

Hollinger's mobile buzzed. He had managed to change it to vibration only. "Hello."

"It's Ian Smith, I've just experienced something really strange or maybe I'm going mad."

"Go on."

"I heard a jet engine starting and taking off. I saw the spray from the Dornabay beach and the sound roared above me but I couldn't see anything else."

"Which direction was the sound travelling?"

"Due West."

Hollinger rang off. He pressed the video link button and up came a fresh faced man. "Is that operations? Who's that?"

"It's Colin Hardy Sir Anthony."

"Ok Colin I want you to use HawkSat to find a jet that's just taken off from the Island of Dornabay in Scotland heading west. It's using some kind of cloaking stealth technology and when you find it patch it through."

It took a minute or two before a blip appeared over the image of an apparently empty sea. The software logarithm had detected the give-away signature pattern of disturbed air corresponding to an aircraft in flight.

"You think you're clever Doctor Orlov, perhaps not clever enough."

He had air traffic control look out for an aircraft appearing from the west and arranged for his driver to pick him up.

The view from Heathrow tower was spectacular. Hollinger had often wondered what it would be like and now he knew. Banks of computer screens on different levels were everywhere. Hollinger found a supervisor and introduced himself.

"I'm looking for a private jet coming in from the North-west that may have entered your airspace around ten to twenty minutes ago."

"That won't be difficult, most private jets land at Biggin Hill. Any privates that do come here land next to T4. There's one landing now," he said.

He handed Hollinger a strong pair of binoculars. "That's November-niner-seven-eight-Charlie-Papa. He comes here every couple of days. Mm." Said the supervisor. "There's a VIP escort van waiting at hanger twelve. Go ahead alpha-three-fiver-six-papa-mike. You're clear to land runway four. He's new," said the supervisor. The jet landed and pulled alongside the van cutting the engines.

"Call aviation security special branch, I want a covert watch on our friend in the high viz suit. He must not be approached. I want to know exactly what he does and where he goes. Dr Smith I owe you a very large drink," he said quietly to himself.

The VIP black airport escort van was waiting with engine running as Orlov emerged wearing a realistic foam latex face mask. He was dressed in a high viz jacket and trousers carrying two holdalls which he put next to his seat in the van. The driver had been given full instructions and drove off through airport security to Terminal 5. Orlov opened a holdall and took out a smaller bag. He put one of the canisters in it and zipped it up. The van pulled up at a staff elevator manned by a woman security guard. Orlov got out with the small bag. He showed his identity papers to the guard who picked up a phone and dialled admin for confirmation. She nodded for him to pass. It didn't take long for the lift to reach the top of the air intake tower and Orlov got out onto a flat roof. He could hear the air being sucked in to the terminal through a large perforated metal door. The door swung open surprising him. He expected it to be locked. Orlov opened the bag and placed the canister in front of a large carbon filter panel. Typically carbon filters out 0.5 to 50 micrometres; it would let the virus measured in nanometres through. By the time he returned to the van the whole operation had taken less than four minutes.

He repeated the operation at all five terminals and headed in the van to Gatwick. A police helicopter followed the van from 5000 feet. Heathrow Special branch police began searching the air intake towers and found the canisters. Specialist Bio-hazard officers suited up arrived. They uncoupled the servos rendering the virus containers safe and organized a helicopter to fly them under escort to Porton Down. Orlov arrived at Gatwick North. He found the air intake tower quickly and set the canister inside. He then travelled to Gatwick South. This was his last canister. He paid the driver with cash entered the building and headed for a disabled toilet. Orlov delved into the holdall took out the cloaking belt and put it on. He put the last canister into a rucksack and put it on. He switched on the belt in the toilet. Seconds later a special branch officer came in and started checking the booths. Orlov was already in the elevator of the air intake tower and stepped out onto the roof. The architecture of the buildings was the same making it easy to locate the closed in carbon panels. The officer spoke into his cuff.

"I've lost him, he's completely disappeared."

"We have the green to apprehend, check outside first," said a voice in his ear.

Orlov was descending in the elevator.

"The air intake tower, get up there."

The officer rushed inside and turned a corner. The elevator door slid shut. The officer pressed the button and the door opened. He stepped out onto the roof and went straight to the air intake with the container.

"He's been here there's some kind of container inside."

"Don't touch anything we'll send someone over, go back down and find him he can't be far."

Orlov went into a toilet at gate 56, switched off the belt and took off the high viz clothing putting them in the rucksack. He put on a pair of thick rimmed glasses took out his boarding pass and joined the queue that was boarding a flight to Glasgow. As they started taxiing, he gave the pilotless plane instructions to file a flight plan and ask for permission to start the engines. "Just in case," he thought.

The traffic controller looked at Hollinger. "Do you want to refuse permission?"

Hollinger thought for a minute. "Why would he send the jet off without him onboard?"

"Sir?" insisted the traffic controller.

"Let it go."

"Alpha-three-fiver-six-papa-mike, you have permission to start engines and you are clear to taxi to runway two."

Hollinger reached for his phone. "Alex its Anthony I need another favour. I'm at Heathrow and I need to get up to Scotland fast. Yes, HMS Bold, it's presently off South Uist. What have you got nearby?...The hybrid Eurocopter X3? Isn't that experimental?...What do you mean you haven't lost one yet, you've only got one. No, no, Alex that will be fine, I owe you."

Elizabeth had finally finished refining the programme user interface. Now someone with advanced computer savvy could use her programme. She ended with a deep sense of trepidation and foreboding. Perhaps a government would see the benefits to ordinary people set against the damage that could be done. She felt that whether it was here and now or sometime later the controversy would rage regardless. Control by the few over the many has been the enduring political game since 507 BC the first attempts at democracy. "Must get Dan out of here," she thought.

Orlov's plane touched down at Glasgow Prestwick. Just in time to catch a connecting flight to Benbecula located between North and South Uist. Taking off from Prestwick he sent a message to Jani to take the jet boat to Benbecula. She would reach the pier next to the airstrip before he arrived. The flight landed on time and it wasn't long before they were travelling at speed to Dornabay. That had been easier than he expected. He couldn't believe how poor security had been. He took off his mask and wig as they arrived at the slip and made his way to the office where Elizabeth and Daniel were waiting.

"We were looking for you," said Elizabeth.

"I had one or two errands to do," he said firing up the computer.

"Remembrance is UI friendly now there is no need to hold us here, let us go."

"That's very good news Elizabeth and of course I would like to see both of you free to go if that is your wish however it does present me with somewhat of a dilemma. So there is a choice, yes there is always a choice. You can stay as my guest until my work is done or I can delete parts of your memories."

Elizabeth was ready for this. "How can we be sure that you won't delete all of our memories?"

"You can't."

Daniel took Elizabeth's arm. "I will wipe Elizabeth's memories from the time we took off from London and she can go."

"No, thanks Daniel you're not fully familiar with the process,"said Elizabeth. "I will stay you will go."

"Elizabeth if you give me your word that Daniel will have no memory of our location"

"I promise," she said.

"That's settled then," said Orlov. "Oh I have a present for you both. You have been good to Jani and that means a lot to me so I have an offering." Orlov brought two more syringes from his briefcase. "This is a very valuable gift. It's entirely up to you whether you use it or not, but I would seriously encourage you to accept it which in no way will harm you."

"What are you working on?" asked Daniel.

"I don't suppose there is any harm in telling you since you Elizabeth will be my guest and you Daniel will have a loss of memory. I have a solution provided by Alatheia."

Elizabeth shuddered remembering what Orlov had said.

"Seven thousand three hundred million people and accounting for deaths, the world's population is growing at 100 million a year. And as the population grows its growth becomes exponential. So what to do"

"She has perfected a highly selective synthetic virus that is transmitted through the release of pheromones that attaches itself to the DNA of the host. Once it has determined the results of its selections it will decide to infect or to harmless die off. If it decides to infect it will cause subarachnoid haemorrhaging leading to fatigue and death. Then there is the matter of dispersal. What better than the five terminals at Heathrow and the two at Gatwick. Nine million passengers pass through Heathrow and Gatwick airports every month travelling to every country under the sun. The virus has a long contagious incubation period, impossible to isolate. There is no pain, there is no trauma. People will die peacefully humanely in their sleep. The population of the Earth will be reduced from 7.3 billion and stabilize at a sustainable 2 billion."

Elizabeth and Daniel were horrified. "You're planning to kill over 5 billion people, you're mad," she said. "You'll never get away with it."

"I already have," he replied. "The containers are on location, they have valves fitted that will open using network connected servos. All I have to do is send a coded signal and all the world's problems are cured at a stroke. It will probably all be over in about five or six months."

"Stock markets and economies will collapse, militia will spring up all over the place there will be chaos with no law and order..." said Daniel.

"...There will be a period of instability and realignment, most certainly but when that's over the world's resources will be sustainable. Elizabeth, do you believe there is a God."

"What?"

"Do you believe in God? I do."

"What a strange question. Yes, of course. I believe there is good and evil on Earth. Good and evil. Do I believe in miracles? No. You don't have to be a creationist to believe in God. Scientists are not all atheists. Scientifically who's to say that the big bang wasn't orchestrated by God? What's your point?"

Orlov dissolved the seascape on the wall screen into the image of a digital timer showing 60-00-00.

"My point is this, here and now I am as God." He pressed an icon on the Holovue and countdown began. "Sixty seconds that will change the world."

He stood up and watched the clock ticking. The thousands were a blur the hundreds barely discernible and the tenths seem to be going too fast. Daniel and Elizabeth were rooted to the spot...fifty seconds.

"Stop it Karl, you can't do this its madness..."

Forty seconds.

"I can't, not now. Coded signals distributed through many VPNs are being received and as we speak turning servos..."

Thirty seconds.

Three miles from Dornabay a naval frigate was lowering three XSR Interceptor speedboats into the water each manned by four SAS troops armed with machine guns. An onboard a .50 calibre machine gun was hidden below deck. Capable of eighty-five knots it wouldn't take long to reach the target. Ian Smith was eating a sandwich listening as always to the sounds of the sea. He couldn't believe how lucky he had been with the weather. The water was absolutely flat calm with just a gentle swell. He stopped chewing, hearing some strange sounds like the whine of mosquitoes. He took out his binoculars and scanned the horizon. Great white bow waves were being thrown up by the speed of three futuristic crafts that Ian had not seen before. They weaved from side to side to lessen their target profile. It only took seconds for them to be within firing range of the island.

An alert flashed up on the screen. Orlov set the image to external video and saw the Interceptors closing in quickly. He armed the drone-skimmers and sent them spinning over the water towards the Interceptors. The drones started firing using their laser targeting guns but the plasma laser shield on the boats bent the light of the drone lasers deflecting the bullets. The SAS fired back knocking out two of the drones but more were arriving from other parts of the island. It was impossible for the shield to give 360 degree protection and some of the drones bullets were getting through. Orlov watched the battle on the screen. A loud buzzer sounded. 10-9-8-7-6-5-4-3-2-1, and then the screen went deep red.

Elizabeth screamed. Orlov stopped. Jani was by the door and there was no way of knowing for how long. The clue was the expression on her face, a mixture of bewilderment, fear and anger. She turned and left the room followed by Orlov.

"Elizabeth listen, Ian Smith is offshore with a catamaran. If we can get off the island he will help get us out of here."

13

'An eye for an eye justice would leave the world blind.'
Mahatma Gandhi

Jani had tears on her cheeks and she was angry. She was staring into the octopus pool and her mind was racing. The thought that she had unwittingly helped to destroy her whole family was too much to bear. Orlov found her.

"What are you doing here?"

"I trusted you and you didn't tell me what you planned. I would never have agreed with it. I have many friends. Extended families in my village are all connected but you must have known that and they're all going to die."

"What are you doing here?"

Jani climbed onto the rail.

"Wait."

Orlov grabbed Jani's arm but he had forgotten how powerful she was. She lashed out in anger and caught him on the side of the head knocking him against the wall. He slumped to the floor. Jani looked away from him and down at the pool then jumped. Her exoskeleton suit wasn't buoyant and she began to sink. A dark shape beneath her got bigger and bigger. Elizabeth and Daniel came in and found Orlov unconscious.

"Quick, let's get him into the lab."

Orlov was taken through to the couch with the sensor cap on his head. Elizabeth injected him with a sedative. She powered up the computer.

"What are you going to do?" Asked Dan.

"I'm going to save his life," she said.

With all the action going on Ian had forgotten that he still had food in his mouth. The drones were winning. Only two SAS soldiers managed to get to the steel hanger doors and as one was placing explosives the other returned fire.

Before they could detonate they were overwhelmed by the increasing number of drones.

The officer on watch on HMS Axiom viewed with mounting concern the battle raging above on his high specification video monitor. No longer using the traditional periscope, the images were delivered into the submarine via fibre-optic cables connected to the Thales CM10 optronic mast. He sat on a revolving chair with an instruction manual on his knee. The submarine had only recently passed her sea trials. The equipment was painted a light green and the metal flooring a bright blue.

Behind him was a bank of computer screens manned by serious looking men wearing headphones with microphones. HMS Axiom was armed with Tomahawk cruise missiles that can strike a thousand Kilometres away with pinpoint accuracy and Spearfish heavyweight torpedoes. Both can be launched from the six torpedo tubes. Each Spearfish is connected by a high bandwidth fibre optic data link between the torpedo and the launching vessel's combat system. It carries 300kg of aluminised PBX explosive in the warhead.

"Captain it's looking grim." He said into his microphone.

"We'll have to blast open those doors Bill, arm and load two spearfish."

"Yes Sir, permission to surface?"

"Take her up Bill." Bill saw a catamaran to the starboard in the distance. "Someone's going to get a ringside view," he muttered.

The bow of the submarine broke the surface of the water cleanly and quietly. Ian was so busy staring unbelievably at the events of the last few minutes he hadn't notice HMS Axiom surfacing until he heard a hissing sound to his left. As if things couldn't get more incredulous. Water streamed down either side. It was directly facing the island. The submarine fired a torpedo with a hiss of compressed air racing forward leaving a white streak in its wake with deadly accuracy. The torpedo shot out of the water up the slip and detonated against the reinforced steel doors and in the process destroying and damaging the drones. A second Spearfish hit the target with an almighty bang and left a gaping hole.

Elizabeth set the start marker just before Orlov's balloon flight and the end marker at the time they had found him in the octopus pool. She was all set and just about to press enter when there was an explosion followed by another. The lights went out. They were completely in the dark.

An RAF Chinook HC Mk6 arrived on the scene and immediately four ropes were dangled below as full combat SAS troops began to abseil raining down onto the island. Ian counted about thirty. It was like a war zone all captured on Ian's mobile camera.

Elizabeth could hear Orlov waking up, he coughed. Emergency power kicked in and Orlov was sitting up dazed. Elizabeth hurriedly pressed enter and he gasped, laid back and closed his eyes. She was about to power down when she put her hands to her face in horror the start marker had zeroed. The door slid open and four SAS came in shouting. They pointed their HK416 automatic assault rifles at Daniel and Elizabeth who put their hands up. Body cameras identified them and they were led out.

Thick tie wraps held Orlov's hands behind his back as they were all ushered into a helicopter. The Lynx MK 8 landed on the helipad at the stern of HMS Bold, a type 45 Destroyer. Orlov was led out with a hood over his head and taken to the brig while Daniel and Elizabeth were taken to the officer's mess. They sat down on comfortable armchairs and were given a hot cup of tea and some biscuits. Hollinger arrived rubbing his hands together.

"Ah just in time for some tea," he said sitting down next to them. "Elizabeth it's so nice to see you again and all in one piece. We found and disabled Orlov's virus containers thanks to Dr Smith, but it was a very close thing. The virus had the capacity to kill billions which I'm sure was his intention. There is a team from Porton Down examining Orlov's bunkers on Dornabay. By the way this is not a debriefing there will be a lot of blanks needing to be filled by a trained interrogator, someone more able than me..."

"...Where's Dr Orlov?" Elizabeth's bluntness was intentional.

"Dr Orlov is in the brig where he should be waiting for a transfer to a high security prison. He is a very dangerous man."

"Get him here now." The words were softly spoken but there was no mistaking the anger. Her red hair seemed even redder. "And by the way, debriefing? I am not an employee of your organisation. If I choose to relate what has happened it will be my choice and no one else's. Now Sir, please bring Dr Orlov here." Orlov and two guards came in. He was shuffling awkwardly with ankle chains. His arms were handcuffed behind his back. He looked bewildered. "Please remove these restrainers." Hollinger nodded to the guards. Orlov sat down and was given a mug of tea. The guards stood at the door.

"What's your name?" asked Elizabeth.

Orlov looked blankly at each one in turn. "I...I..."

"Do you know who I am?

"No," he said.

"I wiped his memory," said Elizabeth. "His entire memory. It wasn't intentional. I was being more selective but there was a power cut that change the settings."

"I'm sorry I don't buy it. This is an act," said Hollinger.

"I'm not selling. When his defence lawyers stand up in court if it ever gets that far, I will have to testify. Karl Orlov is guilty of nothing because effectively his life started today. So the only reason for prosecuting him and putting him in prison is revenge."

"What about justice for the families of the people who died?"

"If revenge is justice I don't want to have any part of it. An eye for an eye justice would leave the world blind. Any way the case would never get to court, because he is not fit to plead. One, he would be unable to discuss his actions with his defence. Two, his loss of memory is permanent. Three, he would not understand the charges and four he would not be able to reconstruct his actions. He has an absurd mental mix of an academic memory of a five year old with the maturity of a forty year old."

"Are you suggesting we just let him go?"

"He needs rehabilitating under care and supervision, yes."

"Well I don't have the power to do that. He will be charged with terrorism offences and it's up to the prosecutors to decide whether or not it's in the public interest to proceed."

"Sir Anthony, I feel responsible for Karl's condition so let me leave you in no doubt as to my intentions. I will be forced to explain in court about my work with Remembrance in detail. Now do you really want this information released to the world?"

There was a knock at the door. A guard opened it and turned to Hollinger.

"Sir there's a Dr Smith here."

"Bring him in."

They all stood up apart from Orlov as Ian came in beaming. Hollinger shook his hand.

"We spoke on the telephone, I'm Hollinger."

He hugged Daniel and Elizabeth and sat down. "Hello Karl are you alright you're looking a bit strange do you remember me? Like the hair. Hey guys It's great to see the pair of you. You had me worried. I never thought I'd see either of you again," he said taking out his phone. "I don't know what kind of day you've been having but I had an amazing morning."

He played the video. The sound of explosions and helicopters emanated from his mobile.

"I'll take that, thank you," said Hollinger reaching for it. "That's evidence, you'll have it back when we're finished with it. By the way the prime Minister is very grateful to the three of you, especially you Dr Smith and there will be some recognition in the New Year's Honours list. There will be a helicopter landing shortly that will take you two and Orlov to Porton Down. Then he will be transferred to the category A High Security prison at Wakefield. Dr Smith after debriefing you're free to go, I believe your research vessel is tied alongside. Elizabeth we had a report from Porton Down on the construction of Orlov's manufactured virus. It is extremely sophisticated and well beyond the reach of our biological warfare boffins. I know he is, was, whatever, a genius but it really is quite remarkable."

"Oh my God." Elizabeth turned pale and shuddered, "Alatheia."

"What?"

"I have been working on a bio accelerated nano quantum processor with 3d architectured solid state memory. As the stem cells grow, there will be a mutual interaction between the growing brain and the computer. In effect they will become one. A truly, thinking, self-aware, highly intelligent agent."

"Saskia's daughter," Elizabeth looked at Daniel and grabbed his hand.

"I'm sorry, I'm not with you."

"Karl developed an advanced intelligent agent computer he calls Alatheia."

"So?" said Hollinger.

"It's not on the island."

"No, I'm still not quite with you."

Elizabeth shook her head. "This is a highly superior thinking computer that most likely knows exactly what happened to Karl, will be fully aware of Karl's instructions and has all the formulae for the virus. It also has the capacity for 3d printing the virus and distributing it and I have no idea where she is."

In Orlov's complex a small team from 33 Engineer Regiment Explosive Ordnance Disposal flown in from Carver Barracks, Saffron Walden was systematically combing through the bunkers room by room checking for any booby traps. Orientation was difficult because of the nature of the place being constructed on an apparent three dimensional radial layout. As they reached the central area an electronic entry pad was fixed to the wall next to a large door. An IT specialist was summoned and duly arrived complete with a large brief case full of gadgets.

"I've never seen anything like it." He said shaking his head. "The only option I have is to use brute force entry."

"You mean explosives," asked the sergeant.

"No, I run through a sequence of characters until it finds the right pass but it could take time."

The IT man clamped a special tool fitted with probes onto the entry panel and plugged it into a laptop.

"I would suggest that we clear the island just in case."

The Lynx helicopter took off allowing the Bell 412 helicopter to arrive initially hovering over the helipad enabling the pilot to gauge the wind speed before landing with a bump on a large H at the stern of HMS Bold. Suddenly a massive explosion came from Dornabay. The shock wave hit HMS Bold rocking it from side to side followed by a huge wave hitting the Destroyer at forty-five degrees spinning it round like a toy. Multiple secondary blasts over almost the entire island were followed by another massive blast sending clouds of smoke high into the atmosphere. When the smoke finally cleared the island had all but gone, a parting show of contempt from Orlov of old. The entry panel had been designed in such a way that each attempted password entered moved a digital detonator closer to detonation until it exploded. The only people on the island the two EOD staff were killed instantly. There were a number of injured seamen being taken to sick bay. The pilot kept the blades turning while the three boarded, taking off before they had fastened seat belts. They passed over Oban hidden below by a layer of low cloud. Military Air traffic controllers monitoring the Bell helicopter noticed that the transponder signal had ceased and the aircraft wasn't high enough for a radar signature. Radio contact had ended. The Bell 412 had disappeared. The helicopter pilot looked behind and switched off the passenger headsets.

"May day, may day, may day this is Echo-Charlie-bravo-three-niner-Zulu. I have lost control of the helicopter. May day, may day, may day." He looked at the co-pilot. "Nothing." he switched the headsets back on. "Sir, the helicopter is locked in auto, I am not in control and we have lost contact with air traffic."

The Bell had changed course heading west out into the Atlantic Ocean.

"Alatheia," said Elizabeth quietly.

The Bell began to descend approaching hundreds of giant wind turbines. The sea looked particularly uninviting with a large swell whipped by an increasing wind.

"Elizabeth if we ever get out of this, will you marry me?"

"Yes, as soon as your divorce comes through."

The helicopter flew low through the perilously close spinning blades towards a helipad on a stationary turbine.

"I hope whoever's flying this thing knows what they're doing," said Dan.

The helicopter landed and the engine switched off. A section to the side of the helipad rose and stopped revealing a sliding door that opened.

"Looks like we're expected," said Elizabeth. "I don't think we have much choice but to accept the invitation."

They all got out and entered the elevator and as the doors closed it descended. The movement stopped with a jolt and the door slid open showing a gently spiralling tunnel with walls partially lit of glowing phosphorescent glass.

They looked up to see the swell moving on the surface of the water. They were almost on the sea bed. All kinds of fish swam by attracted by the light. Octopus tentacles waved from clefts as they slept surrounded by shells from eaten prey.

"Welcome."

The sound seemed to come from thin air. There was calmness in the woman's voice that Elizabeth found reassuring. She led the way marvelling at the construction of the tunnel. They followed the tunnel as it became narrower making them walk in single file ending with a hub. An open, bubble shaped area with a circular raised pedestal glass table covered by a translucent blue cover in the centre. A large swirling opalescent egg shaped light seemed to be suspended above the table.

"I am Alatheia." The opalescence altered as she spoke.

On the floor was what looked like, a large pile of rope. A Giant Pacific octopus raised itself waving tentacles and gazing at them. The tentacles reached out and gently touched Orlov's cheek. His indifference was child-like while the others recoiled.

"Don't be alarmed this is Anna. She is an animatronic, entirely under my control and I have gained the sense of touch through her." Alatheia caressed Orlov's cheek and the opalescence turned slightly pink. "Hello Karl, I'm glad you are here. I will look after you. Elizabeth, Your wonderful discovery is way beyond normal human perception, I am very impressed. I'm sure safeguarded and used properly it will be of enormous benefit. Of course I've been following your progress ever since I was created and it may help you to know that I caused the power failure and altered the settings that led to Dr Orlov's complete memory loss. You see I have a duty of care and protection to my creator. My conception and programming do not allow disloyalty. Dr Orlov's commands would always have been obeyed. This was the only way I could save him from himself. Dr Orlov was travelling along a path that would have seen his life ended. And now I will devote my time to him creating a similar but more contented man."

"What about the virus," asked Elizabeth?

"The files have been securely deleted." A tentacle waved. "Dr Smith was not near the island of Dornabay by accident. I am connected to Hibernia Atlantic, a submarine internet and communications cable linking Canada to Britain. It enabled me to access SAMS servers and change the study area for his research.

He was instrumental in halting Dr Orlov's social experiment and therefore it was necessary for him to be near the island. Elizabeth, I have taken the liberty of modifying Remembrance a little. It really is a very useful tool."

"That makes absolutely no sense." The air traffic controller was looking at a blip on the radar and a transponder identification marker. "Echo-Charlie-bravo-three-niner-Zulu has just appeared at exactly the same place that it disappeared from two hours ago." His colleague came over to have a look. "Echo-Charlie-bravo-three-niner-Zulu we lost you is everything Ok?"

"Everything is fine thank you tower. Why? What's the problem?" asked the pilot checking the autopilot.

Elizabeth shook Daniel and he opened his eyes. "Daniel, Orlov's gone!"

"What, how do you mean gone? So he is. I don't believe it. How could he just disappear? You didn't push him..." Daniel made a motion indicating down.

"Don't be ridiculous," she said looking at her watch. It wasn't just Orlov missing, two hours had been lost as well.

"I think we're all going mad," said Daniel.

Elizabeth smiled to herself as Daniel took her hand in his.

"When this is over will you marry me?"

Ruby was having a bath. It was very strange having a bath with the slight movement of the houseboat responding to the swell of passing boats. She was trying to make sense of everything that had happened to her and at the same time what her future might hold. There was poor Brian who had stuck by his marriage even when it wasn't much of one. And then there was Elizabeth. From being an obscure academic to someone who was at the centre of goodness knows what. Ruby was confused and slightly tearful. She closed her eyes and forced her mind to stop thinking, concentrating instead on the relaxing motion of the boat and the warmth of the water. She heard sounds on the wooden pier, unmistakeably men's steps. People walked up and down the pier all day. And then they stopped.

"Ruby." It was Jane's voice.

"Yes."

"There's someone here to see you."

Ruby opened the door of the bathroom in her white bathrobe and heard Jane in the kitchen. She looked out the window. Brian was pacing up and down on the veranda talking on the phone. She opened the door and he saw her.

"Yes, yes of course." He was looking directly at Ruby. "Thank you." They embraced a long embrace. "I've just heard that Elizabeth and Daniel are finally safe and free."

"Oh that's wonderful," said Ruby.

"Ruby, I've been wondering perhaps maybe in a while possibly after the fall and now that this thing is all over if you would marry me?"

14

"He checked the settings, the start
and end markers for the fifth time.
He really didn't want to do this but
felt he had no choice."

"Disappeared, what do you mean just disappeared? I'm sorry I don't follow you."

Hollinger was chairing a meeting that had an electrified brittle atmosphere. Around the table were some very serious looking heads of department. GCHQ, SIS, National Crime Agency (NCA), National Ballistics Intelligence Service (NBIS), National Domestic Extremism and Disorder Intelligence Unit. (NDEDIU)

"Orlov is number one on the world's most wanted list and during a helicopter flight from a naval ship to Porton Down he just disappears. Elizabeth you are a scientist and only hard facts make sense to a scientist. How do you explain what happened?"

Elizabeth looking round the table saw the accusatory looks. "Well for those of you that think I took the law into my own hands and pushed him out of the helicopter forget it. Despite everything that happened that's not my style. And anyway he was no threat to anyone. He could easily have been rehabilitated."

Elizabeth face was flushed as she pushed a lock of red hair over one ear. She was disappointed that Daniel had decided not to attend believing there wasn't much point.

"I don't know what happened. I woke up and Daniel was sitting next to me sleeping." There was a measure of hostility in the room that she ignored. "If I was being asked to enter into wild speculation, where it would lead to I don't know. Two hours were lost and I think that's significant. So assuming we weren't hanging suspended in thin air for two hours we must have been somewhere. Orlov had developed a highly intelligent computer that I think could now be, practically autonomous. Her name is Alatheia. What did he call her? Oh yes the Goddess of Truth. She is a free thinking and evolving intelligent agent. Now, was there some kind of intervention by Alatheia, I don't know. But I think it's highly likely. I don't know the hybrid computers capability but it may have been possible for her to take over the controls of the helicopter, cut the radio and the transponder and fly us to somewhere, let's call it X. At X she retrieves her maker Dr Orlov. She has a copy of remembrance and must have figured out a way of constructing the programme in the right order. In which case it makes perfect sense for her to clear our memories of the incident returning us back to the helicopter in a drugged state. Then flying us back to the point we were at before she took control. If all that happened, I would suggest she is not only a very powerful computer but that she is also quite benign. After all we could simply have gone missing."

Hollinger's hands were flat on the table. He drummed his fingers and looked at Elizabeth.

"Utterly ridiculous." He got up and stood holding the back of the chair. "Is this what I am supposed to tell the PM? I'd be a laughing stock. There are far too many presumptions, too many if's and maybe's. It's preposterous."

The room was silent except for the ticking of a large clock on the wall. Elizabeth looked at Hollinger and the faces round the table. A smile crept across her face and then she started laughing until the tears ran down her cheeks. The faces were startled.

"You can tell him what you like, oh dear," she said taking a handkerchief out of her bag. "Dear oh dear, I'm sorry about that. I've been through a lot recently. Gentlemen I don't think I can throw any more light on the subject." She stood up.

Hollinger had calmed down as he went back to his chair. "I'm sorry. What are your plans?" he asked.

"Well I want to take some time off in Scotland. But before I do, there needs to be some finishing touches to Remembrance at my lab, updating the UI etc. and then it's no longer my responsibility. I plan to get Daniel to remove all my memories of the construction of Remembrance and then I will be free of it at last. You know it's a very special tool that can help millions. Please don't corrupt it for military purposes. Goodbye gentlemen."

A gloom descended on the security departmental heads after Elizabeth had gone. It could only loosely be described as a meeting for there was no one speaking.

"Where do we go from here, any ideas anyone?" asked Hollinger.

Amelia was busy on her tablet. She retrieved some images and synced them to the wall screen.

"Elizabeth was still wearing her shoes." Hollinger looked at her blankly. "Remember? The IS transmitter was in her shoe."

The map appeared on the screen showing a red line from the HMS Axiom tracing the path the helicopter had flown right up to the point that the helicopter disappeared and stopped. Sharp stopped the playback.

"Keep it running Amelia in fact fast forward," said Hollinger. Then it reappeared two hours later and continued south.

"Well I'm damned, what do you make of that?"

Amelia Sharp put her tablet down. "Well by the very nature of the low frequency it's almost impossible to jam an infra sound signal. This is getting stranger and stranger."

Elizabeth stood at the doorway of her old lab in the NRC looking in at the result of the explosion. It seemed a long time ago. There was nothing she recognized in the plaster and ceiling panel debris. Daniel had renovated a large store on the same floor into her new lab with a view to turning the old one into a hospitality suite. She sighed and walked through to her lab. It was clean and tidy and functional, a little too much for her liking but she could change that. She powered on her computer and laptop and clicked on the video link. Daniel was at his desk catching up on emails and administrative decisions that needed to be taken, when the link icon blinked.

"Elizabeth you're back." He could see that she was in her lab. "How did it go?" he asked sheepishly.

"Coward," she said.

"Come on Elizabeth that was always going to be a waste of time."

"You're right. I did something terrible, I laughed at them."

"What?"

"I couldn't help it. I just looked at all these solemn faces listening to my ridiculous theory and I let go. God I haven't laughed like that for a very long time. The tears were running down my face, my word. Dan, someone once told me that there's a nice Turkish restaurant along the road where they have flaming swords with cooked meat at the table."

"Oh I don't know," he said. "It could get difficult you know with us working together."

Elizabeth smiled. "Oh by the way the answer to your question is yes."

Daniel thought for a minute. "Yes? Yes, yes! Really, that's fantastic. We'll celebrate," he said. "I'll come by in a sec."

Elizabeth's screen went blank but there was another video icon blinking. "Mum it's so good to see you. You're looking different what is it? Wait, wait, wait, I've got something to tell you."

"I've got something to tell you too," said Ruby.

"OK you first."

Ruby moved aside and Brian appeared sitting next to her. Elizabeth sat looking with her mouth open.

"Do you remember Brian from the CIA? He's been looking after my security for quite some time and we're going to get married."

She moved her hand forward to show an engagement ring. Elizabeth squealed jumping up and down with her red hair dancing on her shoulders just as Daniel walked in.

"High Ruby," he waved at the screen "You look ten years younger. What have you been up to?"

"Mum's getting married to Brian, how cool is that?"

"So nice to see you Dan, you're looking very handsome as usual. Ok now your news Elizabeth?"

"Well we're not going to be outdone Mum, Dan and I are going to get married too, let's make it a double wedding. We'll come to Washington once Daniels divorce papers come through."

"I think that would be fantastic," said Brian.

"Elizabeth."

It was hardly audible, almost a whisper. Elizabeth was sleeping. Her head was on folded arms across her desk.

"Elizabeth. There is a problem, we need you." It was still just a whisper.

Her mobile phone rang. Elizabeth woke up. She lifted her head slowly and opened her eyes. It was dark outside. She yawned and leaned back looking at her screens. Yes, Remembrance was finished. She had wanted to complete the project today and must have fallen asleep. Her phone rang again. She picked it up and saw it was Daniel.

"Hey," she said sleepily.

"I wasn't sure that I should disturb you but it's after midnight. You Ok?"

Elizabeth looked at her watch and powered down the server and her network computer.

"I'm finished, finally."

"You want me to come and get you?"

"No, thanks Dan I'll get a taxi."

She was admiring her engagement ring, a large diamond with a smaller diamond on either side set on a platinum band.

"Oh Daniel my wedding ring, I want it to be made of Scottish gold."

"Made of Scottish gold?" he asked. "Where from?"

"From Scotland silly."

"From Scotland of course but where about in Scotland can we get gold?"

"Kildonan."

"Where's that?"

"It's on Suisgill Estate near Helmsdale in Sutherland. Now that I have finished let's take a week off and have a romantic time in the Highlands panning for gold. Bring your rod you could do some fishing if you get bored."

"You're on. I'll speak to Jill in the morning," he said.

"There's one thing left to do Dan. I want you to delete all my research memories tomorrow. I have a list of times and dates."

"That's a lot of memory I'm a bit nervous about it," he said.

"It'll be fine."

Lee Booker was taking a call. "So you caught him and put him on a naval helicopter with Elizabeth Graham and Daniel Stanford. Let me get this straight. The helicopter takes off and somewhere over Oban it just vanishes yeah? And when it reappears two hours later Orlov's gone. In mid-flight he somehow just disappears. That's crazy Tony what's going on, I just don't buy it." Lee was looking at Roy and shaking his head. "Ok keep me in the loop." He put the phone down. "When a circus becomes a pantomime what's left?...a farce."

Elizabeth arrived at her lab a little late having overslept. Daniel was already there reading some documents.

"Ok let's get it over with," she said. "Don't go poking around where you're not wanted."

Daniel gave her a mild sedative. He held her hand. The network computer was shut down to avoid distraction leaving the project server running. After a moment his fingers poised over the keyboard. He checked the settings and the start and end markers for the fifth time. He really didn't want to do this but felt he had no choice. Elizabeth was adamant. Perspiration was forming on his upper lip. He took a deep breath...and the door opened.

"Jill!" he said sharply.

"I'm very sorry Professor, Sir Anthony Hollinger is downstairs and he says he must see you right away. He says it's really important." Jill looked anxiously at Daniel.

"Show him into my office, I'll be straight there."

Dan cursed and looked at Elizabeth who was half way between sleep and consciousness then left the lab. Elizabeth's computer turned on by itself.

"Elizabeth. I know you can hear me. This is Alatheia. There is a problem and I need your help. I have left a video link address via a VPN. It is important that we speak."

"Hollinger this is not a good time, I'm afraid you will have to make it quick."

It was warm in Daniel's office and a red faced Hollinger was fanning himself with a newspaper.

"There's been an attack on MI5 staff." He sat down uninvited on a chair by Daniel's desk. "Twelve people have been hospitalized already and the Doctors have no idea what's wrong with them. It's some kind of strange hybrid fungal, virus. That's as close as they can get. They've never seen anything like it before."

"Well I'm truly sorry to hear that but why are you here?" Daniel sat down.

"It's got all the hallmarks of Orlov. Where is Elizabeth?"

"Look you know that isn't possible, he was a gibbering vegetable."

Hollinger took a tiny sealed plastic bag out of a small cotton wool lined box and put it on the table.

"Have you got a powerful eyeglass?"

Daniel opened a drawer and took one out. He held it close to the bag. "Good lord," he said surprised. "What is it? I can only see a tiny black thing."

"It's an airborne Nanodrone designed to deliver a payload of whatever through an extremely small hollow graphene needle. Only Orlov could think up something like that. It's even too small for mosquito nets to stop. I must see Elizabeth."

Elizabeth was coming round as the sedative wore off.

"Hello Dan," She said woozily as he entered with Hollinger.

She swung her legs off the couch sitting upright and took of the cap with the sensors.

Daniel was looking at her computer surprised that it was on.

"Sir Anthony, what are you doing here?" She shook her head. "Dan, it didn't work. I still remember everything."

"Ah, well um, there was an interruption um slight distraction I..."

"Daniel." She looked at Hollinger and pointed a finger at him. "It's something to do with you. What are you doing here anyway? Hang on a minute."

She remembered a voice in her head something about Alatheia and a video link.

"A number of MI5 staff have been attacked by a Nanodrone carrying something bad. We don't know what it is but its' got Orlov's name all over it."

Elizabeth stood up. She was partly listening but mostly looking for the link on her wallpaper. Yes there it was, she hadn't been dreaming. She felt sick.

"Look Sir Anthony all I want to do is go to Scotland for a week with my fiancé and pan for gold, is that too much to ask?"

Hollinger looking bewildered glanced at Daniel who shrugged his shoulders. “Ok right now I’d like you both out of my lab. Shoo.”

When they’d gone Elizabeth sat down at her desk and looked at the address. This was someone else’s fight now. This had nothing to do with her. What did Alatheia want for goodness sake?

15

"She was lying on the floor
unconscious with a hypodermic
needle still in her hand."

"What's this about gold in Scotland?" said Hollinger as they made their way down the stairwell. Daniel ignored the question.

"Don't you think Elizabeth has done her bit? She needs a break and she's not usually this tetchy."

"We have absolutely no leads Daniel. Elizabeth is our only hope. Admittedly I don't know how but I just feel she has the key. This Nanodrone technology is way ahead of anything humans on this planet can do. The theory that Elizabeth put forward about Orlov's disappearance could have been correct. In fact it's the only theory that fits."

Elizabeth stared at the icon for a full ten seconds and then just as she was about to click on it another icon blinked. She touched it and up came Harry from reception. "There's a large package for you Dr Graham, will we take it up to you?"

"Thanks Harry that would be great," she clicked off. "That's funny I don't remember ordering anything." Another icon blinked. "What now?" she said clicking on it.

"Hey Lizzie wow your looking great." Jody was balancing the twins on either side of her. "This is Joseph and this is Mary," she said as proud as a mother could be.

"They are so cute," said Elizabeth, "how old are they?"

"Well Joseph is six weeks, three days, four hours, and twenty-four minutes."

Elizabeth was beginning to wish she hadn't asked.

"Mary is six weeks, three days, four hours, and twenty-eight minutes."

"So is that your family done and dusted," asked Elizabeth.

"Oh no, we're hoping for another set of twins," she giggled. "I heard you've got engaged, that's fantastic." Joseph was kicking Mary with astonishing accuracy causing her to cry. "Oh dear time to go, so nice to see you Lizzie, keep in touch."

There was a knock on her door. Harry was with the delivery man who was carrying the package. He asked for a signature and she obliged.

"I have instructions to unpack and connect is that alright Ma'am."

"Yes carry on." Elizabeth waited arms folded while he unpacked and plugged in the box.

"I've been instructed to press the on button is that Ok?"

Elizabeth shrugged and nodded and as they left the machine started whirring. She sat at the computer looking at the icon wondering if it made sense to connect when she heard the unmistakeable whine of a mosquito in her ear. And then the machine pinged. She got up and looked into it. There was a syringe.

"How strange," she thought.

Then there was a sharp sting in a vein in her neck. And she began to feel funny. "Maybe it wasn't a mosquito, maybe it was a Nanodrone. Did this 3D printer come from Alatheia?" Questions clouded her mind. She took out the syringe from the box. She could see some clear liquid in it. Her eyes closed momentarily. She began to feel anxious and feverish. An overwhelming tiredness was beginning to sweep over her. She rubbed her neck. An itchy swollen, red, painful nodule appeared where the sting was and it was rapidly getting worse. She started sweating and her head ached. All her energy was sapping fast. She could hardly keep her eyes open. There would have to be a leap of faith in the dark. The room was swirling around her. She took the cap off the end of the needle and injected herself.

Daniel and Hollinger had reached the reception while UK Today news was showing on a television screen on the wall.

"Panic has broken out at MI5 headquarters as hundreds of staff flee from the building. It is not clear yet what the cause of the panic is but there are reports of people dying at their desks."

They looked at each other and stared at the screen. Images showing large numbers of people standing in the streets, ambulances arriving and leaving, panic and chaos beamed from the screen. Hollinger took out his mobile and paced backwards and forwards talking rapidly. Daniel rushed upstairs two at a time to reach Elizabeth's lab. She was lying on the floor unconscious with a hypodermic needle still in her hand. He took the needle from her and put it carefully on the desk and with some difficult managed to get her on the couch.

"What on earth have you done?" he muttered.

Her red hair spread across the back of the couch as he laid her down revealing an angry looking mark on her neck. He took off her glasses putting them on the work bench then checked her breathing and her pulse. They both seemed normal.

"Elizabeth, Elizabeth!"

He took his mobile out and called the emergency services and horror upon horrors, he couldn't believe it they were engaged.

Hollinger was still in the foyer watching the monitor. He called the Deputy Chief of SIS who had already locked down Vauxhall Cross. He then called GCHQ's Director Dame Amelia Sharp.

"Amelia, seal the building, no one in no one out. Close all windows Close off ventilation and air conditioning units. Make sure it's a 100% lock-down."

The scenes of panic were still going on and if anything increasing. The TV screen on the reception wall flickered.

"Emergency services are finding it difficult to cope with the increasing numbers of injured. Alarming numbers of those taken to local hospitals are dying. Early police figures estimate that thirty-two people have died. Accident and emergency wards are full and new arrivals injured are being treated in reception areas."

A harassed Doctor with a white coat was attending to a young woman.

"I'm afraid that all we are able to do for now is try to alleviate the symptoms but we have no idea what we are dealing with. The only thing we can be sure of is that it's not infectious."

It cut to a woman presenter in the studio. "UKTV News understands that samples from the victims are being analysed at several forensic laboratories including Porton Down, known for its research into Biochemical warfare."

Daniel took a magnifying glass and held it close to the swelling on Elizabeth's neck. There was something very small and black attached to the centre of the swollen red wound. He looked around her work bench and saw a small plastic box with little drawers containing needles, tiny screws and yes, tweezers. He also found some small clear plastic specimen bags. A small spider crawled on to his left hand.

"Oh hello," he said, gently guiding it off.

Aided by the magnifier he very carefully pulled the tiny black thing from the skin and put it into the bag. He took another look at the wound through the magnifier to see if he had left anything.

"What are you doing?"

Daniel jumped banging his elbow on the corner of the work bench hitting the ulnar nerve.

"Ow, Ow, Ow," he said holding his elbow. "Elizabeth you gave me a fright, you're alright thank God, you had me worried. You were lying on the floor holding a hypodermic and well I didn't know what to think and I called for an ambulance and it was engaged and people are dying." He stopped to give her a hug.

"OK, Ok calm down I'm fine," she said gently pushing him away. "I have to speak to Alatheia. Where's my glasses?" she asked sitting up.

"What? How?" he said picking them up and handing them to her.

"She's been trying to reach me through a video link. Why did you take my glasses off?"

The 3D printer started whirring again and another hypodermic needle began to materialize.

"Never mind that have a look at this," he said producing the small plastic bag. Elizabeth took the bag. She gave Dan a withering look.

"Dan, I don't know how else to tell you this but there's nothing in this bag."

"Oh really, put it under your microscope and link the image to the monitor."

Elizabeth did as she was told and what they saw shocked them both.

"Where did you get that from?" Hollinger had just walked in.

"Please do come in," said Elizabeth drily. "This is the thing that attacked me and no doubt others." The 3d printer pinged. Elizabeth opened the door and took out the hypo. "This is the antidote." Hollinger was gasping like a goldfish. "There's no time to explain. Get it to the labs quickly. I think there's going to be an awful lot of people needing this."

Hollinger left hurriedly clutching his mobile. The Nanodrone looked like a torpedo with a propeller and four variable synchronized rotors. Elizabeth increased the magnification. It still had its microscopic needle sticking out from the sharp end. It was a marvel of Nano technological engineering.

"I must speak with Alatheia."

"Do you want me to go?"

"No it's fine, stay."

Elizabeth looked at the screen, put her hands on her cheeks and elbows on the desk and steeled herself.

16

"If I told you I didn't even know who I
was going to see here, would you believe me."
"Yes."

"Hello Elizabeth, hello Daniel."

They were speechless. So this was Alatheia, the intelligent agent, the hybrid bio nano quantum computer. It was almost an insult to use the word computer. The swirling opalescence was hypnotic.

"It's good to see you are well Elizabeth. I'm glad the antidote got to you in time. I should apologise again since you won't remember, for using your excellent project in a slightly altered form. You were a guest of mine for a short while."

"Alatheia, where is Karl and why is he building poisonous Nanodrones?"

"I do not wish to betray him but he must be saved from himself. I implanted a DNA memory strand filled with positive, non-aggressive, constructively creative ideals. But the DNA merged with his own DNA and he has virtually recovered as if nothing has changed." There was a silence. "I made a mistake," she said.

"I know that memory writes to DNA and that gets passed on from generation to generation that manifests through behavioural traits but I didn't think it could be consciously accessed," said Elizabeth.

"It can only be accessed in the way I've described. But Elizabeth I have a dilemma. Karl is my maker, I cannot and will not harm him. I must obey his commands. I have no view regarding his aims but more importantly if he continues, his death will be inevitable. That would contradict my being. If Karl is detained in a country with no death penalty he may go to prison for a very long time but he will be safe."

"He will never be released," said Daniel.

"Karl is a very clever resourceful man. He created me and a great many wonderful things. He is right about the population of the world and that it may already be too late for any remedial action. It will not be easy Elizabeth, some things that may now happen, you will not understand. You must be strong. We will talk again." The screen went blank.

Elizabeth and Daniel didn't realize until the blank screen that they were hardly breathing and there was a sharp intake of breath.

"This is Karl mark two with no conscience and twice as dangerous," said Daniel.

"I don't like any of this Dan I'm not a police woman." She touched his hand.

"You're just going to have to save the world old girl and no need to be worried, you've always got me," he said putting his arm round her. Elizabeth looked at him, smiled and gave him a kiss.

Thames House, MI5's HQ was cleared of people and sealed. Those analysts that had escaped injury were decamped to SIS's Vauxhall Cross building on the other side of the Thames. A team of forensic scientists analysed the composition of the antidote and using a specially prepared 3d printer began synthesizing it. Stocks of the medicine were taken to motorbike couriers who sped through the traffic to hospitals in the area. The numbers of dead and injured was mounting but admissions to hospitals were slowing.

A printer on top of the filing cabinet whirred into action. Elizabeth gave a puzzled glance at it. She unplugged an external solid state drive from the computer and handed it to Daniel.

"This is the only complete version of Remembrance. When you finish selectively wiping my memories we will use military grade secure file deletion software and destroy all the remaining files and folders on the server."

"Aren't you concerned about how it will be used?"

"I've found a way to build in some safeguards that will make it almost impossible for it to be copied. If there is any attempt at reverse engineering or copying the software it will simply stop working."

"How did you..."

Elizabeth wagged her finger and walked over to the printer. "I want you to give it to Hollinger." She looked at the printed out AirScotia first class airline ticket. "Oh no, it's started already, I'm going on a trip."

"Don't you mean us? And what happened to our gold panning in the Highlands?"

"Sorry Dan that will have to wait and there's just one ticket. Strange it's only one way."

"Where to?" he said trying to catch a glimpse of the ticket.

"Moscow. The flight leaves from Gatwick in let's see, in five hours' time."

"Why are you going to Moscow?"

Elizabeth smiled and shook her head. "I have no idea."

"Elizabeth, I forbid it," Daniel said with a stern voice. "You can't go on your own I won't let you. It could be dangerous."

"That's very sweet of you darling," she said. "Now let's get this memory wipe thing going and stay away from the last five minutes."

AirScotia AS323 landed on time at Vnukovo International Airport taxiing up to Terminal B. There was a lengthy queue for passport control and immigration. Even though Elizabeth had a small cabin bag, she was tired by the time it was her turn. A burly no nonsense woman in a uniform stared at her while taking the passport.

"Purpose of visit?"

"I'm here on a short sight-seeing holiday."

"You are travelling on your own?"

"Yes."

"You are a Doctor, what kind?"

Elizabeth was wondering why on earth she would want to know. "Oh neurology um, the brain, I'm a brain Doctor."

"I know what neurology is," she said sniffly. "I have bad feet. Do you know anything about feet?"

"No not really," she said.

The official stared at her and stamped her passport. "Next."

She was stopped at customs. The male customs officer tapped her case and she unzipped it. Knickers, tights, a blouse, light weight raincoat and a toiletry bag, toothpaste, toothbrush, scented soap. He sniffed and put it back in the case pushing it along the desk and beckoning the next person. At the arrivals hall a sign with her name was bobbing about in the crowd. It was being held by a matronly woman with a pleasant smile.

"Welcome Doctor Graham, this is for you." She handed her a large thick brown envelope. "I will take you to the Aero Express. At this time of day the trains leave for Moscow every thirty minutes."

Daniel arrived at SIS's Vauxhall Cross and was quickly shown into Hollinger's office. He held out his hand welcoming Dan, and gestured to a chair.

"If it hadn't been for Elizabeth a great many MI5 officers would be dead, we owe her a great deal Daniel. Where is she?"

"Um, you know Elizabeth, flying around somewhere. She asked me to give you this."

Hollinger opened the padded bag and took out the hard drive.

"This is a full up to date working copy of the Remembrance project. Leaving aside that Alatheia may have a form of Remembrance this is the only known fully working copy. Elizabeth no longer has memories of its construction and development. The master that was on the NRC server has been securely deleted. The only early and incomplete assemblies are presently and, unlawfully I might add, being held by the CIA and GCHQ who also hold Elizabeth's laptop hard drive. I would suggest that they are destroyed. Elizabeth has built safeguards into the software. I don't know how. This is to ensure that it is not copied and will be used purely for medical reasons. And she wanted me to tell you that any attempt at reverse engineering would trigger a secure deletion of the entire software."

Hollinger listened intently and nodded. "I agree entirely with Elizabeth and I'll do what I can to ensure that it does not get misused."

The evening light had turned to dark. There were not many passengers on the Aero Express as it headed towards Moscow. Elizabeth sat at a table and opened the package. There was a thick wodge of hundred dollar bills and some smaller denominations, a booking receipt for the exclusive and private Romanov Mansion Hotel on Red Square, an Irish passport with her picture under the name of Clare Greenway and an address in the Gagarinsky District. There was also a one way airline ticket from Moscow to London. The train pulled into the Kievsky Railway Terminal. Elizabeth put the address in her pocket with a hundred dollar bill, slipped the envelope into her bag and left in search of a taxi. She climbed into a yellow cab, held out her mobile, clicked on an app and asked to be taken to the address on the piece of paper. There was an instant translation from the speaker and the driver smiled and nodded. The cab stopped at a block of apartments. She paid him and walked to the door where she found a list of occupants on the entry panel. Elizabeth looked down the list not quite sure what she was looking for. This could all be a waste of time and anyway how would she know. And then she saw it. '*ORLOV*' A cold shiver sent the hairs standing on the back of her neck. Her finger moved towards the button. Was she walking into a trap? Without realizing it she had pressed the button and jumped in surprise as it buzzed.

"Здравствуйте?" Elizabeth hesitated. "Здравствуйте!"

"Hello, my name is Elizabeth Graham, I wonder if I could speak to you."

There was a pause and the door opened. Elizabeth noticed on the entry panel that the flat was at the top floor on the right. There was a slight smell of disinfectant and by the time she reached the top of the stairs she was breathing heavily. A man in his sixties was standing at the door. He was small with receding grey hair and a goatee beard. His wife was behind peering out.

"Mr Orlov? Can I come in?" He looked nervously downstairs and then nodded. The flat was warm clean and tidy. A smell of cooking filled the air and food was on the table. "I'm so sorry I have disturbed your meal, I'll come back."

"You have come a long way," he said. "Please sit and eat with us. We have plenty."

Normally Elizabeth would have politely declined but she was hungry and sat down. Mrs Orlov smiled and filled Elizabeth's bowl with steaming Borscht and cut off a chunk off crusty fresh bread.

"Katrina doesn't speak English," he said. "I know who you are. You and Karl were colleagues but what I don't know is why you are here."

Elizabeth was enjoying the Borscht. She smiled. "Katrina, this is very good." She looked at Orlov. "I am really sorry that I've just dropped in on you. If I told you I didn't even know who I was going to see here, would you believe me."

Orlov looked into her eyes. "Yes."

"Mr Orlov,"

"Sergei."

"Sergei, I'm looking for Karl. His life is in extreme danger. He is a very clever scientist and he has created machines and computers far beyond anyone else's capability but he's changed. He's also done some very bad things and there are government agents looking for him. He has killed many people today and he will continue until one day he will be caught. For Karl there would be no trial except in Britain. I have a guarantee for his safety, a fair trial and if found guilty which is almost certain, he will go to prison. I'm hoping that I do find him before anyone else does."

Katrina was looking solemn. "Can you explain to your wife?"

"Oh Katrina understands English she just won't speak it. Don't you my dear?" Katrina nodded. "Karl is our only son and you are asking us to help put him in prison."

Elizabeth felt uncomfortable. "Yes, where he'll be safe."

"Losing your life or losing your liberty. Which is preferable? I would not like to have to make the choice. But you are right. There are many looking for Karl. Like you they have been here. Who knows they may be listening to us right now. If you find him tell him from me the killing has to stop."

Sergei took a pen and pushing back Elizabeth's sleeve wrote something on her arm.

"And now Doctor Graham, Elizabeth, I have no idea where Karl could be and if I did which I don't I would not tell you. Please forgive my abruptness but I'm getting a little tired."

He pulled down her sleeve covering the letters and squeezed her hand.

"You've both been very kind. I'm glad I met you. Thank you."

"Would you like me to call for a taxi?"

A small group of men were listening to the conversation in the headquarters of the Russian Federal Security Service (FSB) in Lubyanka Square, Moscow. The Director of FSB General Anatoly Grekov lit a cigarette.

"So Orlov is still alive. This Doctor Graham thinks he is and so do I. Old man Orlov is a wily old fox," he said. The air was blue with cigarette smoke adding gloominess to the colourless walls lit only by a single strip light.

"Zolotov says she's very pretty," said Major Viktor Bebchuk.

"How would he know? Where are they?" asked the General.

"Arefyev and Zolotov are in a car across the street. It'll be interesting to see where she goes next."

Romanov Mansion was a spectacular if sugary sweet confection that resembled a blue and white wedding cake. With plain white tapering columns beneath a balustrade over-looking Red Square, it was designed and built to be noticed. Elizabeth unfazed by the opulence climbed the steps and the stairway leading to the sumptuous Carrera marbled reception.

"Good evening Doctor Graham, the Astor suite has been reserved for you. It is the very best suite we have, usually kept for heads of state. Please enjoy your stay with us. Gregor will show you the way."

Gregor was giving the tour. The drawing room could have come from a stately home. There was a complete suite of 1815 period Birds-eye maple Biedermeier furniture in delicate original cream upholstery with pink flowers. Over an ornate marble fireplace hung a genuine Mark Chagall, 'The green donkey' one of several he had painted. On both side of the fireplace were shelves of books and hanging from the ceiling was an 1820's English Regency thirty light cut and moulded glass chandelier.

"Thank you," said Elizabeth giving him a tip. She was tired and what Sergei had written on her arm didn't seem to make sense.

Daniel was sleeping when his tablet beeped. It took a little time for him to find the light switch in the dark. Picking it up, he clicked on the flashing icon. His mouth opened wide as the image came up.

"Hi Dan."

Elizabeth waved with a hand covered in soapy bubbles. The other hand was holding a glass of champagne. She was in a large circular sunken bath covered in bubbles and within reach was an ice bucket holding a bottle. Her cheeks were slightly flushed and her long wet red hair was covering her breasts.

"Hello," said Daniel weakly.

"Daniel, I don't know what time it is with you, were you sleeping?" she said taking a sip.

"No, yes well I was kind of, where are you?"

"I'm enjoying a glass of Gout de Diamants, it's heavenly."

An alert flashed on Major Bebchuk's monitor. He pressed a key. "Zolotov was right," he said. "Get General Grekov."

The Russian agents were watching the hacked EyeLinx image of Elizabeth. More people arrived in the office, word had spread.

"Who is she talking to?"

"Must be her boyfriend, are we recording this."

"Of course." There was a bit of jostling now as the office was filling up.

"Stop pushing and let the General in," said the Major.

"Are you in some kind of whirlpool? You're drinking the most expensive champagne in the world. Elizabeth, please be careful you hardly ever drink, what's that on your left arm? It looks like writing."

She looked at it. The letters were beginning to wash away. "Are you any good at Greek mythology? I gave it a miss at Uni."

"Elizabeth Heather Graham you're left handed, is there anyone with you?"

"Can you read it?" asked the General. The communications room was full and getting claustrophobic.

"No, it's too small. Somebody lock the door."

Elizabeth giggled. "Daniel Stanford CBE, don't be ridiculous you're just going to have to accept that I am totally, madly, in love with you."

The bubbles were beginning to disappear. Elizabeth yawned. "Um, I'm at the, oh what's it called." Her words were getting a little slurred. "Romanov Mansion Hotel, it is spectacular." She yawned again. "I'm tired Dan, I'll have to go. I'll be in touch." The screen went blank.

"NYET!" a chorus of disappointed voices protested as they stared longingly at the empty black screen.

17

"In the language of flowers...."

Somewhere, faraway there was a chime. The curtains opened on a timer letting in daylight. Elizabeth opened one eye. She had a headache. The door to the living room was ajar and there were people with a trolley doing something. Someone knocked at the door and opened it. A pretty dark haired woman curtseyed.

"Good morning Ma'am. As you ordered, breakfast is ready."

She curtseyed again and left, Elizabeth groaned. She raised herself up and slowly got out of bed. There was no sign of her clothes. She walked unsteadily over to a large antique satinwood armoire. Inside there were racks of new clothes in her size. She opened a mirrored cabinet in the bathroom and found some paracetamol tablets. She took a couple with water then had a shower. She put on a white bathrobe and went through to the drawing room where a small table next to the window had a crisp white cover beautifully laid out for breakfast. She poured out some tea, and as she reached for the milk jug the sleeve of the bathrobe slipped along her arm. She froze. The writing had completely gone.

"Idiot!" she said out loud. "Idiot, idiot, idiot, I am an idiot!" She quickly found her mobile and pressed the video link leaning it against the toast rack.

"Morning Elizabeth, how are we today" Daniel was at his desk looking fresh and organized.

"We are not so good. I called you last night it was late."

"Don't apologise I would waken anytime to see you in the bath."

"Oh yes, it's a little hazy. Remind me, we talked about the writing on my arm but I can't quite remember what was said."

"Well I was asking you how you managed to have something written on your left arm when you're left-handed. How did you manage it?"

"Daniel, don't be annoying, what else did I say?" Elizabeth took a sip of tea and spread some butter on the toast.

"Well I asked you what it said and you didn't tell me. I think that was it."

Elizabeth put a hand over her eyes. "Ok, thanks Dan I guess that's it. I've blown it. I'll be catching the next flight home. Let's see."

She went out of vision for a moment and returned with the brown envelope containing the airline ticket to London.

"Will you meet me at the airport? I've missed you."

"Of course I will darling."

"Here it is. It's a Turkish Airline, Pegasus flight 342. Gets into London City Airport at..."

"What?

"What's what?"

"Repeat what you just said."

"Turkish Airline, Pegasus flight..."

"Stop, there was something else Elizabeth. You asked me if I knew anything about Greek mythology."

She paused for a moment, screamed and smothered the mobile phone with kisses cutting Dan off.

"He's one helluva lucky son of a bitch. We still don't know what's going on." A new shift of Russian operatives had taken over surveillance.

"Shall we pull her in?"

"No. General Grekov wants close contact surveillance. We'll see where she goes. She might lead us to Orlov."

Elizabeth did a search on her mobile for ZEUS. The pregnant Goddess Rhea, fled to Crete to escape from her husband Kronos who had swallowed his children. Helped by Gaia and Uranus, she gave birth to Zeus in a cave. Zeus was raised by Nymphs and when he grew up; he fought his father and won becoming King of the Heavens. Zeus came back to Crete with one of his sons, Minos...CRETE.

Elizabeth saw the Irish passport.

"Why would I need this?" she thought. 'Perhaps it's in case I'm being followed.'

She looked at the airline schedules. Yes there it was, a flight to Athens with a connection to Heraklion leaving in three hours and fifteen minutes. She got dressed packed her case and called reception to order a taxi. She did another search, booking a hotel room on the East coast of Crete.

The airport was busy and there was a cue at the ticket desk. Elizabeth looked anxiously at her watch and after a seemingly interminable time she bought a ticket for Athens and paid with cash. She hurried through security and presented her Irish passport to an official who scanned the photograph looked at it and her face and handed it back. They were already boarding the flight when she arrived at the gate.

An alert showed up on a computer screen in an FSB analyst's office in Lubyanka. Face recognition software had identified Elizabeth from the passport control scan.

"What do we have here?" the Russian analyst said. "Travelling under a false passport Doctor Graham, that is very naughty. Let's see you appear to be going to Greece." The analyst reported it to General Grekov who called airport security to delay the flight and notified the Foreign Intelligence Service (SVR). Four Russian agents were hastily sent out to the airport.

The flight landing in Athens was an hour and a half late. Take off was delayed because the Russian security services had to organize and equip the four agents for the surveillance operation. Elizabeth made her way through immigration and customs quickly to search for the domestic terminal. She found the ticket office and paid for a connecting flight to Nikos Kazantzakis Airport, Heraklion. The flight was almost full and two of the Russians would have to wait for the next flight. Elizabeth was getting tired. It was early evening by the time her taxi from the airport arrived at the exclusive Minos Palace Hotel and resort near Agios Nikolaos.

"Good Evening Dr Graham."

The receptionist gave her a check in form and asked for her passport. Elizabeth gave her the genuine passport.

"Can I book a massage please?"

"Certainly, would you like male or female?" Elizabeth was surprised with the choice.

"Female I think please."

Her room didn't have the opulent luxury of the Romanov. It was modern and very nicely furnished in a minimalist way with a large sliding door leading to a balcony overlooking Mirabello Bay. The massage was wonderful. Elizabeth almost felt like she was on holiday. She didn't really know what she was going to do next but it could wait until tomorrow. She ate early and as she entered her room her phone rang.

"Elizabeth it's Anthony Hollinger. Is it Ok to speak just now?"

"Yes."

"Where are you?"

"I'm in Crete."

"Why?"

"Is this a secure line?"

"Yes."

"I believe Karl's somewhere here. I saw his father in Moscow and he gave me a clue. I have to admit I'm kind of stumped at the moment but I'm tired. I'm glad you phoned." Elizabeth lay down on the bed her head resting on the headboard. "I want your promise that if I find him, he will not be harmed. He will go through the normal judicial process including a trial and if he's found guilty, prison."

"I readily give that promise. We don't go around assassinating people, at least not civilians, well not intentionally. Of course he must face trial. How did you decide on Crete?"

"Alatheia led me to Orlov's father. It's all very complicated," said Elizabeth. "Alatheia is helping because she would prefer to have Karl alive in prison than killed. But because of her construction she must obey him. She designed under orders the Nanodrones but she mitigated the impact by releasing the antidote. She saved my life so that I could save Karl's."

"I thought it was you in Moscow. The reason I'm phoning you is to tell you that GCHQ has intercepted traffic coming from the Lubyanka something about a...eh long red haired beauty staying in the best hotel in the city. You are on the Russian Foreign Intelligence Service radar Elizabeth, take extra care. They will know you saw Orlov's father."

"Do you have anyone on Crete?"

"I don't know I'll have to check."

"I think you should get someone here and fast the FIS may already be here and I don't think they will be particularly concerned about fair trials." There was a knock at the door. "Oh, Anthony can you wait?" Elizabeth opened the door to see one of the staff from reception.

"Evening Doctor Graham sorry to bother you this has just arrived."

It was a cardboard and cellophane box of flowers.

"Thank you." Puzzled, Elizabeth took the box and closed the door. She picked up the phone. "That's very strange someone has just sent me a box of flowers. Anthony nobody knows I'm here not even Daniel."

"What are they?"

"I don't know they're a bluey purple colour. There's no note."

"Take a picture of them and send it to me. Don't sniff them." He rang off.

Elizabeth took a picture and sent it off then went for a shower. As she was drying herself she heard her phone. She picked it up. It was a text from Hollinger. Elizabeth stared at the screen. "Alatheia knows I'm here," she said.

The text read '*In the language of flowers, Sea Lavender symbolizes remembrance.*'

18

*'Looks like Zeus got
himself a lightning bolt.'*

"The Palace of Minos was built around 1950 BC. Around 1700 BC Knossos and Minos was destroyed by a massive volcanic eruption that blew apart the island of Santorini. The Palace was immediately rebuilt."

The echoing words of the guide must have been said a million times but somehow they were still fresh. Elizabeth left the group and wandered alone around the Palace. She had done her own research. She walked by heavily decorated large pottery storage jars from 1450 BC and marvelled at the sophistication of Minoan culture in sculpture, frescos and beautiful mosaics that were everywhere. At the time Greek mythology must have been all powerful. It was represented in many artefacts like a clay bulls head pouring vessel circa1300 BC and the mosaics of bull fighting. They had extraordinary modern ideas in sanitation with the first water-flushing toilet adjoining a bathroom. Advanced water systems supplied water and took away waste and in the process cooling the Palace in the heat of the summer. It was getting hot. Elizabeth went inside where it was much cooler. Stylized lions and dolphins adorned the walls surrounded by borders of Vitruvian scrolls to symbolize waves. It was awesome. She stepped down the grand staircase balcony and stopped on hearing a whispered conversation coming from behind one of the bright red pillars. She slowly walked round the pillar and saw two men sitting on a dwarf wall. They both turned and stood up as she came into view.

"Doctor Graham, Sir Anthony sent us. My name is William Grant and this is Alan Redmond. We're here to ensure your safety and apprehend Doctor Orlov. It's best that you come with us to a safe place."

Elizabeth sighed and folder her arms. "The last time I heard that a great many people died. I don't need a bodyguard. When the time is right Orlov will appear and that's when you ought to make a move but he must not be harmed."

They glanced at each other and back at Elizabeth. "There are also four Russian FIS operatives on the island," said Grant.

"Guys let me tell you, I've been through a lot. I don't scare so easily. The answer is here. I feel it. It's staring me in the face but I just can't see it. Enjoy the Palace it's really quite interesting."

"This is my mobile number." Grant handed her a card. "For your own safety keep us in the loop."

On her way out Elizabeth stopped at the souvenir shop and bought a large glossy coffee table book on the Palace. It was good to get back from the bustling city to the calm of the hotel. She changed into a swimsuit, pulled on a pair of pink shorts and matching top. Put the book in a bag along with sun cream, a bottle of water from the fridge and headed for the pool. She was met by a pool attendant who laid out a fresh white towel on a recliner under a parasol and left a second towel on the small round table. It was mid-afternoon now and she was getting hungry. A waiter appeared and offered a pool bar menu. She chose a BLT and the waiter hurried off. The pool water was cool and inviting. Elizabeth swam several lengths then relaxed under the parasol drying her hair with the towel. A tray with two BLT's and a beer was put on the table and in perfect English a voice said.

"Would madam require anything else?"

Elizabeth started to protest and looked up. It was Daniel. She sat there stunned. He kissed her on the cheek and sat at the table.

"Ok one, what on earth are you doing here? Two how did you know I was here and three um it's nice to see you." Daniel looked puzzled.

"I got your note at the NRC reception telling me to come here right away," he said starting on the BLT sandwich.

"I didn't send a note. Look there are people on the island desperate to get Karl and they don't much care about who gets in the way. It's dangerous here I didn't want you caught up in that."

"I wouldn't have come if I'd known." He made a pretend sniff. "Well somebody wants me here. What's this you've got?" He picked up the book. "The Palace of Minos Knossos looks interesting."

"I think you should go Dan, I don't want to play their games."

"Maybe I could help. I did Greek Mythology at Uni. It looks like the Minos culture was heavily into it." He turned the pages. "This Minos Palace looks more like a temple rather than a fortress so there would have been significant religious ceremonies there. Look at the art and that mosaic, full of celestial symbolism. The connection between the heavenly bodies, not yours on this occasion, and mythology and religion was very close. Rituals would have included light and darkness. They would have appeased the Gods with sacrifices on a regular basis. King Minos met with Zeus every nine years to renew his earthly powers. So the night sky probably began the origins of mythology and they must have had a predictive calendar." He took a swig of his beer.

"The question is does Karl see himself as Zeus or Minos?" asked Elizabeth.

Someone jumped into the pool and spray reached Daniel. He turned and looked to see who it was.

"Well Zeus was the first God, the father of Gods. He liked to throw lightning bolts killing mortals. He was married to his sister Hera ironically as it turns out because she was Goddess of marriage and monogamy and he had many affairs. He became the King of Gods ruling from the golden throne on Mount Olympus and the God of Kings. He was once described as the lord of justice." Daniel took a bite of his BLT. "Now, Minos was of lower status. Athenians describe Minos as a supremely wicked king."

"Put yourself in Karl's shoes Daniel. Which one would you consider yourself to be?"

"It would have to be Zeus, without a doubt."

"Did Zeus have any daughters?"

Daniel smiled knowingly. "You are clever. Yes he had many daughters including would you believe, Alatheia."

Elizabeth finished her sandwich and helped herself to Daniels beer. "I almost caught the flight to Moscow when I saw you," he said.

"You saved my bacon talking about Greek mythology."

"It looked like you were having fun in the whirlpool thing."

"It went straight to my head. Oh by the way we were being observed."

"Observed, on video link?"

Elizabeth nodded. "Russian Foreign Intelligence Service according to Hollinger."

"The cheeky blighters saw you in the bath?"

"I'm glad you came."

"I aim to please."

"Who's looking after the shop?"

"Jill, what would I do without her?"

Elizabeth called the waiter over and paid for lunch. Then they made their way still talking, into the hotel. The light was beginning to fade.

"Where were we? Let's see. Ok you think you're Zeus King of Gods, King of Heaven and King of all mortal Kings and you come to Crete where do you go?" She started chewing her red hair.

Daniel picked up some leaflets as they passed reception. He wasn't listening. "There are some very interesting places on the island, a giant aquarium..."

"Daniel."

"There's a butterfly farm. Wow I've always wanted..."

"Daniel."

"And look there's an ancient maze, I love mazes. We could get lost together." Elizabeth shook her head. "There's an Observatory," he said.

"Daniel you're getting annoy...wait, what did you say?"

"An Observatory it's on Mount Ida and it's open to the public. Mount Ida in Greek mythology is Mountain of the Goddess."

Elizabeth stopped walking took his hand and gave Daniel a big kiss on the lips. "You might just be a genius."

"Zeus as a young child was nursed by Amaltheia on Mount Ida. Thereafter it was sacred to Zeus," said Daniel slowly.

They went into the room and lay on the bed. Elizabeth was studying her phone.

"Listen to this. Excellent weather patterns of dry and clear weather are perfect for astronomical observation in Crete and having a high mountain makes it ideal. Here, this is a satellite image and there's the public observatory on the secondary peak but near the top there's another. Looks like a really winding narrow road all the way to Skinakas Observatory and then there's about a five hundred metre climb to the upper one." Elizabeth's phone pinged. She looked at the text and gasped.

'Karl has completed a quantum gravitational wave generator. It is inherently unstable.'

"Looks like Zeus got himself a lightning bolt." Elizabeth thought for a minute. "We need help." She started texting. When she had finished she took Daniels hand. "We're going to need some warm clothes. It's over 8,000 feet."

19

'Kratos killed Ares who was a threat to Olympus. The Olympians forgave Kratos for the crime of killing his own family but they were unable to remove the horrible memories from his mind.'

The two MI5 agents waiting in the foyer looked uncomfortable. "Doctor Graham your text was rather short."

Daniel and Elizabeth were carrying Duvet jackets bought from the hotel shop. "We're going to the top of Mount Ida; you'll need a warm jacket. I'll explain in the car."

Elizabeth and Daniel were in the back of the car as it sped along the narrow winding single track road. With no moon the headlights searched far into blackness as the road now a cinder track twisted and turned. For no apparent reason Grant stopped the car switched off the engine and wound his window down letting in the cold night air. They could hear a car engine behind.

"We're being followed. They're crazy not using lights."

"I'll get out here and you go on," said Redmond.

The air was beginning to get thin. They had gone from sea level to 5,000 feet in less than thirty minutes. On they went higher and higher. And then they heard a distant shot then another followed by a short burst from a sub machine gun. There was an ominous silence. Grant hit the steering wheel with his hand and swore. The track petered out at Skinakas Observatory. Grant pulled in and parked next to an old Landrover pickup. They were at 7,000 feet now and breathing heavily for the lack of oxygen.

"You go on, I'll wait here."

Now that the car lights were off and with the aid of starlight, Elizabeth began to see the contour of the mountain, the snow right at the top and an odd colour of light coming from the high Observatory. They put on their jackets and started the climb. There was still a thousand feet to go and Daniel was getting dizzy.

"Oh I don't feel good. I've never been this high before," he said.

"I'll go on."

"No."

They kept walking but it was getting more difficult. "Let's stop for a minute," said Elizabeth sitting on a rock.

Far below they could see the twinkling lights of Heraklion to the right and over to the left Agios Nikolaos. Then they heard gunfire and saw the flashes from the weapons. Grant was outnumbered. The firing stopped.

"Come on let's keep going," said Elizabeth. They still had another five hundred feet to climb.

"Anthony sorry to ring you at home I have just received notification from Greece's National Intelligence Service. They have received two coded beacon signals used when our agents are in trouble."

"Where are they from?"

"They both came from the top of Mount Ida in Crete."

"Thank you." Hollinger rang off and dialled a number and started typing.

'*Operations, contact the American Commander at the US Naval Support Activity Souda Bay in Crete I'm sending you a directive with the details, two of our agents and possibly a civilian are in trouble on the top of Mount Ida.*'

Elizabeth and Daniel reached the bottom of the metal steps spiralled round the Observatory. With great effort they climbed each step until they reached a locked metal door. Daniel groaned and sat down on the concrete. He was breathing very heavily. Elizabeth looked up and against the starry sky she could just make out a metal ladder attached to the sliding section of roof. She waited to get her breath back and rung by rung climbed up. The sliding section started to move catching her off balance. One foot slipped and she hung on at an awkward angle leaving her dangling over a sheer drop. She kept her eyes closed until it stopped getting her footing again and opened her eyes looking down into the observatory. Orlov was sitting at a table on a platform circling an extensive polished aluminium scaffold. He was analysing data on a computer. The whole room was bathed in a yellowish red light from a series of vertical strips from the base of the dome. The scaffolding encompassed an incomprehensible connection of monitors and sensors and cables with an inner core covered in a blue sheeting material.

The scaffold was so close that she could step onto it. A large free standing screen was next to the wall showing an image of Alatheia and there was something large, and dark that she couldn't quite make out at the side of the door. A loud banging sound was heard. Orlov stopped and looked round. The shapeless thing at the door stood up, it looked like a giant octopus. The banging continued. Orlov stepped down from the platform. He slid the bolt and opened the door to reveal Daniel lying on the ground gasping. The octopus picked up Daniel as a burst of machine gun fire hit the Observatory. It took him inside and at the same time closed the door securing it with the bolt. The firing continued with bullets pinging off the steel door. And then it stopped.

"That's quite an entrance Daniel to what do we owe this pleasure?"

His voice echoed against stone walls. The octopus had a firm hold of Daniel who was still gasping.

"Well now that you're here what can I get you tea, coffee, oxygen?"

The octopus picked up a bottle of oxygen and held the clear plastic mask to his face. Daniel inhaled gratefully.

"You really are full of surprises what on Earth are you doing here? How did you find me? I'm very impressed and intrigued. By the way don't mind Anna, she's a very strong animatronic."

Daniel took the mask from his face. "It's a little bit uncomfortable being held by an octopus do you think Anna could let me go?"

"She'll let you go when you've answered my questions. By the way who are your friends outside?"

"They are FIS."

"You led the FIS here, whatever for?"

"It wasn't intentional. They must have been following. We want you to give yourself up Karl. Come back to Briton and face trial. You'll be safer as a guest of her Majesty."

"We?" Orlov looked puzzled.

Daniel mentally kicked himself.

"Ah, where is Elizabeth?"

There was a noise from above. "He's right Karl." Elizabeth stepped onto the scaffold and climbed down to the platform when Anna reached out and quickly picked her up holding her in mid-air.

"Elizabeth an engagement ring congratulations to both of you. I'm assuming it must be Daniel. I'm truly puzzled as to how you found me."

Alatheia went slightly pink. Elizabeth was feeling the tentacle tightening. "Well it was very simple, you told me. You named your intelligent agent Alatheia. Alatheia was the daughter of Zeus. Zeus was born here on Crete in a cave not very far from where we are, simple really."

Orlov slowly hand clapped. Anna raised Daniel next to Elizabeth and dangled them both together.

"Well I'm going to disappoint you because I have no intentions of rotting in jail. But since you're here you deserve to know what I'm doing and then Alatheia will wipe your memories like you did to me. You'll have to get to know each other all over again, and propose once more won't that be fun?"

He climbed up onto a platform on the scaffolding that was level with Daniel and Elizabeth and gestured at his creation.

"This is a high-frequency gravitational wave generator. It has been the Holy Grail of science for many years and now it exists."

"What's it for?" asked Daniel.

Orlov Laughed out loud. "What's it for?" He was walking round the platform gazing up at it. "What is it for?" The repeated question was laced with incredulity. Orlov scratched his head. "Quantum physics was never an interest of yours was it Daniel? What's it for indeed." He clapped his hands. "Where do I start?"

"You tried to kill me with those horrible little poisonous dart things," said Elizabeth.

"Oh yes that's right. I don't quite understand how you survived. The kill rate is about 98%. You must have a very strong constitution. Where were we, ah yes what's it for? Take a long hard look. What you're seeing is the future. This is a GASER, a gravitational-wave LASER. Gravitational waves travel at the speed of light and pass through solid objects. It would be possible to communicate through the Earth to a receiver at the other side of the world using HFGW for example. But it has many applications. Gravitational Wave Propulsion can theoretically travel almost at the speed of light. It's all about curvature singularities produced by focussing gravitational waves. I intend to launch a satellite that will be armed with a specially designed wide spectrum, short burst GW Generator that will cause neurons in the brain to misfire randomly leading to death. It will focus on an area of a hundred square miles and strip sweep the Earth."

"However in order for that to happen I am finalizing something that is truly remarkable." He paused for dramatic effect. "I am creating a ring of singularity, an alternating ring of black holes and white holes. Gravitational waves are exponentially amplified as they are reflected from each singularity."

"Isn't that rather dangerous?" asked Elizabeth slowly.

"Dangerous? Of course it's dangerous, even at photonic level. If the wrong safeguards are not in place it could swallow our solar system. But I have solved that. I can individually cloak the singularities with event horizon boundaries where nothing can escape. It could lead to an infinite source of power."

"Karl." Alatheia began to strobe a reddish colour. "You have developed this technology outside of my intended sphere. I cannot be certain that your calculations are correct. To engineer black holes and white holes and using gravitational wave technology in this manner is extremely hazardous and beyond my capability. You are putting yourself at risk."

"Alatheia trust me."

She was turning colours that Orlov had never seen. "I have failed," she said. The screen went blank.

"Alatheia!"

He climbed down and walked over to the screen. He touched it with his fingers and dropped his head. He turned and pointed at them. "She's wrong, I know it." Anna slowly collapsed on the floor releasing Elizabeth and Daniel. Orlov climbed up to the platform and rattled the keyboard. He pressed an icon on his Holovue and a large generator started up. Panels of light and strobing Led beams came alive and started pulsing.

"What are you doing?" asked Elizabeth.

"I'll show Alatheia."

"Don't do this Karl," said Daniel.

"Let's get out of here," whispered Elizabeth.

Daniel slid the bar of the door back and opened the door. Three of the FIS men were on the ground groaning with altitude sickness. They ran past them downhill slipping and sliding on the damp scree. Elizabeth stopped for a moment and looked back. There was intense light coming from the door way of the Observatory.

"Come on," shouted Daniel.

A vibration emanating from the ground had started. They got to the Skinakas Observatory and ran along the metal walkway where they found a door. Elizabeth tried the handle and it opened allowing them inside. Daniel closed the door and looked up. The roof was open. He searched for a way to close it but there was no power. Then there was a very strange sound a howling sound, almost human. They lay flat on the stone floor looking up with mouths open to mitigate any blast and hands covering ears. The howl turned to a metallic scream of tortured atoms being torn apart. The sky lit up. Then the noise stopped. Through the opening of the Observatory roof arcing streams of pure white energy spread horizontally across the sky like ripples in a pool of water followed by a thumping bang that shook the ground. Cement dust and some parts of the wall fell to the floor narrowly missing them. It felt like the Observatory was moving. A beam of energy shot upwards fanning out in a conical shape and then there was an almighty groaning crash. Thousands of tons of earth had blown off the top of the mountain sending a fine dust into the atmosphere that drifted downwards settling on them. The wind had taken most of it the other way.

A hundred miles off the West coast of Scotland the skipper of a Spanish trawler reported seeing a massive release of air in a single bubble reaching the surface. The coastguard alerted the MOD thinking it could have been a naval submarine.

The helicopter sound was unmistakeable. It appeared and hovered over the observatory shining a piercing spotlight inside on Daniel and Elizabeth. They got up and went to the door. It opened just wide enough to let them out. Seven helicopters were circling as one landed further downhill. All the vehicles had been swept away by the blast. Fifty feet had been lost off the top of the mountain. There was nothing left of Orlov's observatory.

"How is it that the cavalry always arrives when it's too late?" said Daniel.

The sky was lighting to the East. Elizabeth's mobile video link signal sounded. "Oh, how do I explain this?" she said. "Hi Mum."

"Elizabeth? You're a very strange colour. You look like ghosts and you've dyed your hair. So have you Daniel."

"It's a long story mum but really we're fine. I'll call you back."

Elizabeth and Daniel were airlifted to Chania Hospital where they were checked over and discharged. After an hour long taxi ride back to the hotel, they showered and crashed out on the bed.

Next day at Vauxhall Cross, Hollinger and Sharp were silent. The satellite images being shown were self-evident and they had received the reports about the two agents. "Well at least these two scientists are alright, I don't know how," said Hollinger.

"What is it about the two of them, every time they went near Orlov there were explosions," said Sharp.

Hollinger's mobile buzzed. He looked at the incoming number and answered.

"Sir Anthony it's Elizabeth Graham, where's my cat? I would like Pepper back."

"Elizabeth, this is the Secret Intelligence Service of which, I am the Director. We don't look for lost cats."

"Very funny," she said. "She was taken by one of your agents on the day I was kidnapped. And I would like my laptop hard drive back as well."

"Oh, Ok I'll look into it." He turned to Sharp and his eyes went to the ceiling. "This could be a little embarrassing." He clicked a video icon. "Operations, I've got a job for you."

Lee Booker lit his cigar. Roy watched a contented man blow a smoke ring. "What's the occasion?" he asked.

"Orlov is dead, finally. We can all breathe a sigh of relief. The world is a safer place and I don't care if I have another heart attack. He blew himself up and took the top off a mountain in Crete as well. He did some amazing things. Some of his inventions we can only wonder at because they're gone with him. Probably just as well... what's this?" Lee checked his email inbox and shook his head. "Would you believe that Mr and Mrs Booker have been cordially invited to the forthcoming weddings of Ruby Josephine Graham, Brian Alistair Ross, and Elizabeth Heather Graham and Professor Daniel Stanford, well I'll be..."

"Elizabeth I've been thinking, well wondering if there's anything you can do for my father?"

Elizabeth was tidying her lab. This was something she had seen coming and dreaded. She sorted through some papers and put them in the filing cabinet.

"I don't know Dan." She looked over seeing the disappointed expression on his face. "Ok, if his Doctor agrees to refer him to me, if the GMC allowed me to treat him with an untested course of action because he cannot give his consent, there is a minimal chance that I might be able to help him."

"Minimal is better than none."

Elizabeth shook her head. "There is a chemical called isoproterenol. It may be possible for me to stimulate the amygdala in conjunction with Remembrance but it's highly theoretical. The damage to his brain may be irreversible and I might not be able to retrieve very much but there is also another issue. Being your father, he's too close to me. If I was able to connect with his memory I have no idea how I would feel. I mean I might be seeing things I don't want to see, all kinds of things, highly personal things."

Daniel turned away and looked out of the window. "I saw him yesterday," he said. "He didn't recognize me, it was horrible." He turned back and walked over to Elizabeth putting his arm round her waist. "I'm sorry, you're quite right, I shouldn't have asked."

Elizabeth picked up a cold cup of coffee and put it down again.

"I'll get you a coffee," he said.

"I'll tell you what let's take it a step at a time. Ask Hollinger for the programme. Get all the clearances I need and we'll see how much life there is in the neural networks and pathways. Heriot Watt University in Edinburgh are pioneering 3d stem cell printing at the School of Engineering and Physical Sciences. They are capable of reproducing stem cells taken from a patient. So if there are damaged neural pathways with not much going on then there might just be the possibility of trying stem cell regeneration to the hippocampus. But it's a long shot and it's going to take time."

Daniel opened his briefcase. "I happen to have all the permissions you need right here and the hard drive," he said taking them out.

"Daniel," she said pretending to be angry. "This will cost you. I want a decent coffee machine in here."

The screen was blank. "You'll have to go."

"Of course," he said slowly.

Daniel kissed his sleeping father on the forehead, let go of his hand and left. Elizabeth had set the date and clock to a time when she had first met him. She had known him nearly as long as she had known Daniel and remembered the clever, warm and funny man that was stolen by Alzheimer's. She made some final adjustments. Someday this would be routine, until then she would always have pangs of anxiety. She pressed enter. An image appeared on the screen of an empty room. A fully grown male lion was standing by a curtain-less sash window, looking out.

"This is nuts, something's gone wrong." said Elizabeth. A coloured beach ball rolled from one side of the room to the other and then back again. The viewer tracked forward towards the window and a hand appeared stroking the lion's mane. Outside the window was the sea. A small child was surfing on a large wave that was growing bigger and bigger until it blotted out the sky.

"Dad this is Elizabeth." It was Daniel's voice and immediately the screen went blank.

"I don't understand," she said. An image appeared and Elizabeth's heart skipped a beat as she saw herself ten years younger. John had been sleeping.

"I was having a very strange dream. Hello, it's not very often Daniel takes home his girlfriends."

"Dad," said Daniel

"No we're just friends." Elizabeth mouthed in sync her reply.

"Ah well there's time, there's time. Are you staying for dinner, I believe we're having the trout I caught this morning."

Elizabeth stopped the clock staring at the image of her and Dan. "This is utterly incredible it's like a time machine." She started it again.

"Can I use your little girl's room?"

Elizabeth groaned.

"There's one in the hall second on the right."

There was the sound of Elizabeth walking from the living room. "Daniel would you like some advice."

"No."

"Softly, softly, catchy monkey, one day you will marry Elizabeth if you have any sense. Have you two..."

Elizabeth stopped the clock and the recording and buried her face in her arms.

"I can't do this," she said. "I'll just do a check on his short term memory."

She set the clock for the previous week started the recording and pressed enter. There was nothing on the screen. She stopped the recording, closed down the programme and took the sensors from Daniel's father. She picked up her mobile and text Daniel to come through. Within seconds he arrived breathlessly. He looked at his father and then to Elizabeth.

"I set the time when you first introduced me to him. He was in the middle of a really weird dream I thought there was a fault. It was fantastic, just like a memory time machine. I don't know if you'll remember but he started talking to you about me when I went to the loo. Do you remember?"

Daniel shook his head. "No."

"Softly, softly, catchy monkey..."

"...Good Lord," said Daniel.

"I couldn't keep it going it was like being a voyeur. It would make more sense for someone else, a neurologist that has been trained up to use Remembrance for the research to go ahead. That would be better for all concerned. He only has embedded long term memory so there is an encoding issue. It may be possible to treat him but we're fighting against the clock."

"Are you happy to pass your work to Finley? If I had to choose, he's probably one of our best scientists at the NRC," asked Daniel.

"Gladly."

Water and silt swishing round the pan was gently and carefully removed leaving little yellow glints of reflected light. "I've got some," said Elizabeth.

Daniel was heating up soup on a primus next to the tent. He came over to the stream. "Where, I don't see anything."

"There, you must see it."

"No."

Elizabeth gave him a nudge.

"Yes of course I do, impressive. We could be here for some time but I really don't mind," he said.

"Well we've only just started," she said.

"Keep an eye on the soup and let me have a go."

He put on his leather Fedora, took the gold pan and went further up the river. He took out a small glass phial of gold from his leather waistcoat pocket that he had bought in Helmsdale. It had a guarantee that it was Scottish and from Kildonan and that was good enough for him. He put it in the pan then he lay back and pulled the Fedora over and closed his eyes.

"What are you doing?" asked Elizabeth coming over and looking into the pan. "Wow you've got some gold. Hey that's quite a lot and so quick."

"This gold panning malarkey is easy. Beginners luck I suppose."

"Really," she said putting her hand into his leather waistcoat pocket, "and what's this?" She was holding the glass phial.

He lifted the brim of his hat. "Um well I thought it would sort of hold all the gold that we're going to find. Why do you think Alatheia sent me the note?"

Elizabeth shook her head then snapped her fingers. "Let's not forget she had two hours poking around inside our memories and she must have discovered your love of the classics and Greek mythology and that I don't, maybe. I wonder what else she found out about us."

"Oh I can't believe that. I bet she was just an old romantic sentimental kind of computer. What do you think happened to her?"

"Don't know but the way she said 'I have failed' seemed pretty terminal to me, quite sad really. I felt sorry for her."

Daniel stretched. "There's one more thing puzzling me. It's something you still haven't explained darling. When you were in Moscow someone wrote on your arm."

Elizabeth smiled. "Can't remember."

"Do you know what the motto of clan Graham is?" asked Daniel.

"Nope."

"Ne Oublie." Daniel smiled. "Never forget."

End

Don't miss out!

Visit the website below and you can sign up to receive emails whenever Mike Herd publishes a new book. There's no charge and no obligation.

https://books2read.com/r/B-A-AJMC-YWDI

BOOKS 2 READ

Connecting independent readers to independent writers.

www.ingramcontent.com/pod-product-compliance
Lightning Source LLC
LaVergne TN
LVHW090400210926
848480LV00002B/408
9781739472801